Galileo

Renaissance Scientist and Astronomer

Galileo

Renaissance Scientist and Astronomer

Tim McNeese

CHELSEA HOUSE PUBLISHERS

A Haights Cross Communications Company ®

Philadelphia

COVER: Portrait of Galileo Galilei, astronomer.

CHELSEA HOUSE PUBLISHERS
VP, NEW PRODUCT DEVELOPMENT Sally Cheney
DIRECTOR OF PRODUCTION Kim Shinners
CREATIVE MANAGER Takeshi Takahashi
MANUFACTURING MANAGER Diann Grasse

Staff for Galileo
EXECUTIVE EDITOR Lee Marcott
EDITORIAL ASSISTANT Carla Greenberg
PRODUCTION EDITOR Noelle Nardone
COVER AND INTERIOR DESIGNER Keith Trego
LAYOUT 21st Century Publishing and Communications, Inc.

A Haights Cross Communications ⬥ Company ®

www.chelseahouse.com

First Printing

9 8 7 6 5 4 3 2 1

Library of Congress Cataloging-in-Publication Data

McNeese, Tim.
    Galileo: Renaissance scientist and astronomer / Tim McNeese.
        p. cm.–(Makers of the Middle Ages and Renassance)
    Includes bibliographical references and index.
    ISBN 0-7910-8628-3 (hard cover)
    1. Galilei, Galileo, 1565–1642. 2. Astronomers–Italy–Biography. 3. Scientists–
Italy–Biography. 4. Astronomy, Renaissance. I. Title. II. Series.
    QB36.G2M46 2005
    520'.92–dc22

                                                                2005007494

CONTENTS

Early
Directions

In recent years, spacecraft named after Italian scientist and astronomer Galileo Galilei have moved through the darkness of space, seeking new information about the vast universe in which we live. Thousand of years earlier, that same space had remained a strange and largely misunderstood world. During the seventeenth

century, however, Galileo pointed a simple telescope toward the sky and began explaining its
mysteries. It was only one of the worlds he would
help to explain.

The mark Galileo left on science is everywhere
around us today. He affected how we view the
planet we live on, how we look at the stars, how we
understand our solar system, even how we tell time.
Elementary school students today learn the following simple facts about space that we all live by:
Earth is round; it revolves on its axis; it moves
through space in giant orbits; it moves around the
Sun; the Moon's surface is pitted with craters; there
are planets we cannot see with the human eye; the
universe is immense; and the stars are great distances
away from Earth. During his lifetime, Galileo came
to understand the truth behind all of these facts.
He also discovered a way for people to keep better
track of time. Through his experiments, he proved
a swinging pendulum could be used to maintain
clocks at a regular speed, allowing them to keep
more accurate time. This amazing man of the
Renaissance was one of the first in history to understand both time and space.

Galileo's contributions to the understanding of time and space surround us today. He was one of the first scientists to perform experiments to prove his scientific theories.

Galileo was one of the first scientists in history to perform experiments to prove his ideas about the laws of nature. Earlier, scientists who studied the world often invented ideas to help explain the physical world around them, such as the shape of Earth or the nature of the stars. They often created theories using superstition, without a clear understanding of what certain things were really about. Sometimes early scientists were ancient philosophers, people who studied human nature, but their "science" was often wrong. For instance, many early scientists believed that Earth was flat or that the stars were living beings. Most people thought that Earth was at the center of what modern scientists today call our solar system, and that all of the planets, as well as the Sun, revolved around it. They also believed that Earth never moved, but remained in one place at all times. Galileo would prove such ideas wrong.

Several ancient Greek philosophers did get some of their ideas right about the natural world. One Greek philosopher–scientist living almost 2,500 years ago did not believe that Earth was at the center of our solar system, and taught instead that the Sun was at the center. This idea was true, but he had no way of proving his theory. Because he was unable to prove his theory, his ideas were lost for hundreds of years. It would take a modern scientist, such as

Galileo, to prove the validity of this ancient theory. Twentieth-century scientist Albert Einstein called Galileo "the father of modern physics, indeed, of modern science altogether."[1]

Galileo also made certain that his ideas, unlike those of the ancient Greeks, would never be lost. He wanted as many people as possible to know how the world worked. He spread his ideas by being a good teacher and a great scientist:

> He taught his way of performing and interpreting experiments to his pupils and to the nonscientists. In this . . . he was an innovator. He went against the long-standing habit of writing science in Latin for the benefit of the few learned men in foreign countries and wrote instead in Italian, in a pleasant, popular style which almost any literate person could understand. His books, received with great interest and translated into other languages, were and still are models for those who recognize the power of science and its essential place in culture.[2]

Nearly all of Galileo's ideas are accepted today and have remained unquestioned for hundreds of years. During Galileo's lifetime, however, this was not the case. During the 1600s, many of his ideas, especially those about the universe, space, and the planet we live on, were not understood by most people. In fact, his ideas were sometimes considered dangerous. Powerful people tried to stop Galileo from explaining our world. They wanted to believe in the old ideas and old theories in which people had believed since the beginning of time. Some of those people were able to keep Galileo from making his ideas accessible to those who wanted to know the truth. In fact, Galileo was tried in court for his ideas and imprisoned in his own home, but he never gave up seeking answers to the great scientific riddles that no one else had been able to answer. Before he was finished, his studies would take him as far away as the stars.

Test Your Knowledge

1 During which century did Galileo leave his mark on science as we know it today?

   a. The seventeenth century

   b. The fourteenth century

   c. The sixteenth century

   d. The fifteenth century

2 In addition to an understanding of space, what else did Galileo learn a lot about?

   a. Poetry

   b. Weather

   c. Time

   d. Music

3 Galileo was one of the first scientists to

   a. discover that the world was round.

   b. perform experiments.

   c. travel around the world.

   d. discover the theory of relativity.

4 Some early scientists were also

   a. bankers.

   b. lawyers.

   c. philosophers.

   d. musicians.

5 What did most scientists of Galileo's time believe about the solar system?

a. That the Sun was at its center

b. That the stars were at its center

c. That the Moon was at its center

d. That Earth was at its center

ANSWERS: 1. a; 2. c; 3. b; 4. c; 5. d

Born of the Renaissance

Galileo Galilei was born on February 15, 1564, in the Italian city-state of Pisa, located in the rolling hills of Tuscany, in west central Italy. He was the first of seven brothers and sisters born to Vincenzio and Giula Galilei. Galileo's mother and father both came from important Italian families. His father was part of a noble Italian family from Florence. For many years, the Galileis had served as members of Italy's wealthy, ruling class. His mother's family, the Ammannatis, was made up of prosperous cloth merchants.

The world into which Galileo Galilei was born was an exciting one. For most of the century prior to his birth, Europe had witnessed dramatic changes in fashion, the arts, literature, social standards, learning, and the sciences. Historians would later refer to this great period of change and progress in Europe as the Renaissance. Important discoveries were being made during this time. The printing press had come into use across the continent, helping to spur a new age of literacy and books. Less than three generations earlier, Italian explorer Christopher Columbus had sailed west in search of the Far East, only to discover a New World inhabited by people quite different from those of any other continent. By the early sixteenth century, other European sailors had traveled around the vast continent of Africa and had found their way to India. These new connections with distant peoples and cultures brought great changes throughout Europe. The old ways and ideas of the Middle Ages were becoming a thing of the past. The future pointed toward greater understanding and knowledge of the world, beyond Europe's borders. Galileo would one day make his mark on that future.

Italy was at the center of the Renaissance. Many great artists, including painters, sculptors, and architects were Italians—such as Leonardo da Vinci, Raphael, Bramante, and Michelangelo. These artists, as well as dozens of others, helped to create a new style of artistic expression. Their great works could be found in the Italian city-states where these men lived, worked, and expressed themselves, including Milan, Venice, Rome, and Florence. Florence and Galileo's hometown, Pisa, were independent city-states in the grand duchy of Tuscany, situated in west central Italy. Tuscany was then ruled by the most influential, powerful, and wealthy of all Italian families, the Medicis. Medici princes, dukes, and other family members were among the most important supporters of the Renaissance. They helped provide money to artists, scholars, scientists, and other important, creative individuals. Later in life, Galileo would become one of the scientists supported by the Medici family.

Galileo was born during the time of the Renaissance, but he also lived to see the end of this great, productive period in Italian and European history. In the same year that Galileo was born, the great painter, sculptor, and architect of the Renaissance period, Michelangelo Buonarrati, died. Within two months of Galileo's birth, another great European, English playwright William Shakespeare, was born. Men such as Galileo and Shakespeare helped to define the next era in European history. They would build on the emphasis being placed on learning, literature, and the sciences during the Renaissance. Artists, such as Michelangelo, had helped to bring the art world into maturity. It would take men of science, such as Galileo, to help to do the same for the sciences.

FATHER AND SON

Despite coming from two important, powerful, and wealthy families, Vincenzio and Giula Galilei did not live prosperously. The Galilei family, despite its noble roots, had lost most of its money by the mid-1500s. Through his wife's family, Vincenzio Galilei worked as a cloth merchant. He had moved to Pisa from Florence because he believed Pisa was a better trade city for cloth merchants. His real interest, however, was not in Italian textiles, but rather in the world of music. Vincenzio Galilei was a highly educated man, very intelligent, and a lover of music. He not only played several musical instruments, but was also a composer. In his day, Galileo's father became well known for his musical abilities and talents. In time, his work as a textile merchant came to an end and he tried to make a living teaching and playing music.

Vincenzio Galilei was a skilled musician who also studied and wrote about music theory. He created a new style of music as he developed a "revolutionary view of music."[3] Through his studies, Galileo's father became one of the first European music scholars to apply mathematics to the study of music. In fact, Vincenzio Galilei became famous across Italy and beyond for his musical ideas, which he wrote about in public papers read by many other people. Galileo learned many things from his father, including an appreciation for music. Vincenzio Galilei taught his son to play the lute, a stringed instrument similar to a modern guitar. He also

Galileo's father helped to develop in his son an interest in the sciences, including astronomy—the study of planets, stars, and galaxies. Earth and the Moon are seen here from the *Galileo* spacecraft, named after the great scientist.

taught him to play the organ. Vincenzio Galilei's studies also led him to teach Galileo about "the physics of sound."[4]

Although he might not have realized it at the time, Galileo's father also helped to develop his young son's interest in the field of science. During the Middle Ages and the Renaissance, music was considered one of the sciences. Those students who attended the colleges and universities of the Middle Ages studied the seven liberal arts, which included four subjects (the *quadrivium*) called the mathematical arts. The mathematical arts included geometry, astronomy, arithmetic, and music. Vincenzio Galilei's studies combined the latter two—arithmetic and music. As for Galileo, during his lifetime, he completely redefined the study of astronomy. He also developed other qualities, such as taking time for reflection and thought. As a young man, Galileo enjoyed the company of others. He was an outgoing boy, filled with curiosity and enthusiasm, but he also "enjoyed sitting alone in the courtyard or in his room playing the lute or composing his own songs."[5]

Vincenzio Galilei also helped to develop another quality in his young son. In addition to being a well-educated, studious individual, Galileo's father was an open-minded man. He believed in the value of inquiry, the spark that draws curious people to examine things for themselves. He did not believe in simply accepting other people's ideas or explanations. Vincenzio Galilei thought it was important to be skeptical of widely accepted theories and beliefs, especially in the sciences. For this, Galileo's father became known as one who constantly questioned the answers that others blindly accepted. He had little patience for people who were narrow-minded, especially if their ideas were based on superstition, untested religious ideas, or prejudice. Vincenzio Galilei once wrote of his disappointment in those who failed to question the accepted ideas of the time:

> It appears to me that they who rely simply on the weight of authority to prove any assertion, without searching out the arguments to support it, act absurdly. I wish to question freely and to answer freely without any sort of adulation. That well becomes any who are sincere in the search for truth.[6]

Vincenzio Galilei also gained a reputation as a "rebellious thinker."[7] This lesson was not lost on young Galileo. As an adult, his studies and scientific ideas caused many around him to think of him as a rebel, as well. When he went to the university and studied, his fellow students and professors gave him the nickname *"Il Attaccabrighe"*—"The Wrangler."

Cloth merchants usually made more money than musicians and others involved in the creative arts. Because Vincenzio Galilei spent so much time and labor on his music, his family was often short on money. This made life difficult in some ways. As members of two aristocratic Italian families, the Galileis were expected to maintain a wealthy lifestyle. They were expected to dress and live like aristocrats. They were supposed to show off their wealth, but the family often struggled without enough money to live in the manner that was expected of them.

In 1574, Vincenzio Galilei moved his family from Pisa back to Florence. Young Galileo was, by then, a curious ten-year-old boy. The Galilei family had grown. Vincenzio and Giula had seven children in all. Several died young, however. In addition to Galileo, only three others lived into adulthood, sisters Virginia and Livia, and younger brother, Michelangelo. Galileo continued to live under his father's roof for another year. Through age 11, the young Galilei studied under his father, who served as his teacher. A handful of other tutors were also paid to teach Galileo. All of his studies, as well as his other interests, inspired the young boy from Pisa. He was developing into a well-educated, curious young man with many interests. Although he took his studies seriously, Galileo also enjoyed being outdoors, always looking at the world around him through studious eyes. He loved to wander the countryside and explore the rural roads, hillsides, and local rivers, including the Arno. He studied nature constantly. Back in Pisa, "he would go off on his own to discover tunnels and deserted buildings in the city."[8] As an adult, Galileo never lost his spark of curiosity.

Test Your Knowledge

1 Where was Galileo born?
a. Venice
b. Rome
c. Pisa
d. Florence

2 Galileo was the first of how many brothers and sisters?
a. Six
b. Seven
c. Four
d. Eight

3 What did Galileo's mother's family do?
a. They were cloth merchants.
b. They were bankers.
c. They were musicians.
d. They were winemakers.

4 How do historians refer to the great period of change and progress that took place in Europe during the century before Galileo's birth?
a. The Progressive Age
b. The Awakening
c. The Enlightenment
d. The Renaissance

5 When did European sailors travel around the vast continent of Africa to find their way to India?

a. In the fourteenth century

b. In the sixteenth century

c. In the fifteenth century

d. In the seventeenth century

ANSWERS: 1. c; 2. b; 3. a; 4. d; 5. b

A
Searching
Mind

 By the time Galileo reached the age of 11, his father knew it was time to send his young son off to school. Young Galileo, his father understood, was extremely bright and anxious to learn. Although Vincenzio Galilei had taught his son many things, all aristocratic Italian boys were expected to receive a formal education. This created a problem for Vincenzio Galilei, however. Being well educated himself, he was a skeptic of many of those who ran the schools for young men in Florence. He finally decided to send his son to a local Florentine grammar school where he would study for the next two years. At age 13, it was time to place Galileo in his next school. This time, one of his father's biggest problems in determining a school for his son was the family's finances. The Galileis did not have much money to spare for their eldest son's education, thus, eliminating the possibility of sending Galileo to some of the better schools in Florence. Instead Vincenzio Galilei sent his son to a monastery school at Vallombroso, near Florence. The school was run by the monks of the Camaldolese Order, a strict religious group.

At the Camaldolese school, Galileo learned the subjects taught in nearly every preparatory school during the Italian Renaissance. He studied Greek and Latin, languages every Italian gentleman was expected to know. He also learned about logic and the studies of the ancient Greek philosopher, scientist, and teacher Aristotle. Galileo thrived under the direction of the monks. He enjoyed the atmosphere of learning. He also appreciated the quiet lifestyle of his teachers at the monastery. In fact, the young student began to admire the monks so much, he decided to become one. This idea, however, did not sit well with his father, who was not interested in his son becoming a member of the Catholic clergy. Vincenzio Galilei had greater plans for his eldest son. He did not intend for Galileo to take holy vows, or become a merchant, as he had done. Instead he wanted his son to become a medical doctor. After three years at the monastic school, the elder Galilei removed Galileo from the school and took him back to Florence where he was placed, for the moment, under the guidance of a tutor.

The move back to Florence marked one of the first times father and son clashed over Galileo's future. Vincenzio Galilei's plans for his son would not wait long, however. By 1581, when Galileo turned 17, his father placed him at the University of Pisa, with instructions to study medicine. For the moment, Galileo agreed, but he did not remain on track or follow his father's wishes for long. He had other interests. His father had encouraged him to develop his musical talents at an early age, and Galileo also enjoyed writing. Surrounded constantly by Italian Renaissance art, he also tried painting. In his later years, he confided to some of his friends that, if he had been allowed to pursue his heart's desire as a young man, he would have become a painter. Above all of these interests, however, Galileo loved to study mathematics.

Even during his first few months at the University of Pisa, while studying medicine, Galileo began attending mathematics lectures on his own time. One Pisa lecturer and mathematician especially captivated his imagination for numbers, equations, and theories. That lecturer was Ostillo Ricci, the court mathematician in Pisa and expert on Euclidean geometry. (Euclid was an ancient Greek mathematician who invented modern geometry.) As often as he could make the time, Galileo sat in on Ricci's lectures, and Ricci could not help but notice the eager young man with an obvious thirst for geometry. After Ricci's lectures, Galileo would often approach the professor with many questions. Because of the young man's interest and obvious intelligence, Ricci finally suggested that he change his field of study to mathematics. Before the end of Galileo's first term at the university, he had become an undergraduate in the field of mathematics.

Vincenzio Galilei was not happy with his son's decision, but there was little he could do to convince Galileo to change his course of study. This was, after all, the son he had taught to pursue knowledge. Galileo was definitely in pursuit of a greater understanding of not just geometry and mathematics, but also the world in which he lived. The simplest observation might lead him into a whole new world of discovery. One such observation soon set Galileo on the path toward a lifelong study of the laws of science and physics.

The Mistakes of a Great Philosopher

As a student, young Galileo would have studied the writings of those who wrote about science before him. One of the most important figures of study for university students during the Renaissance was the ancient Greek philosopher–scientist Aristotle. In Galileo's day, Aristotle was considered one of the greatest thinkers in world history. He was thought to be one of the most important sources for a clearer understanding of the universe, and the world in general. Galileo used the writings of Aristotle in his studies of logic and of how the universe is structured. Unfortunately, this man, who lived nearly 2,000 years before Galileo, got much of his scientific information wrong.

Aristotle lived during the fourth century B.C. He is remembered as a great philosopher and teacher. (One of his most famous students was the Macedonian conqueror Alexander the Great.) The word *philosopher* means "a person who seeks wisdom or enlightenment," but the ancient Greek definition of the word *philosopher* meant more than it does today. Many of the ancient philosophers were also amateur scientists who tried to understand the natural world. Aristotle studied the world around him so closely that he wrote books on the subject. In those books, Aristotle made some serious mistakes.

Aristotle understood that things wear out and fall apart on Earth, but he believed that the Sun and the stars did not change, remaining, instead, always the same. He also thought that Earth was the center of the universe and that all the bodies in space revolved around it. Aristotle was wrong about both ideas.

He was also incorrect when he wrote that objects in space are always the same distance from Earth, at all times. He theorized that such bodies as the Moon and the planets moved around Earth on gigantic "transparent spheres," huge tracks in space. This idea, too, was wrong.

It is easy to see how Aristotle might have made such mistakes about the universe. He had no scientific instruments and the idea of experimentation was not yet popular. All he could do was observe what he could see with his eyes and try and figure it all out with limited understanding.

Even hundreds of years after his death, Aristotle remained a highly popular man. His writings were considered accurate and unquestionable, but, after a thousand years, much of his writing was lost and many of his ideas were forgotten. Only later, by the eleventh and twelfth centuries, were the works of Aristotle rediscovered and translated into Latin, allowing the theories of this ancient Greek thinker to become popular once more. Once again, Aristotle's ideas were taught as fact. Although some 2,000 years separated Aristotle from the time of the Renaissance, this revival allowed the young Galileo to become one of his students.

A DISCOVERY IN CHURCH

One day in 1583, while at the University of Pisa, Galileo passed through the Cathedral of Pisa, where he attended Sunday Mass. On that particular day, as he sat and listened to the sermon, he became bored by the speaker, a visiting cleric. Distracted, his eyes soon focused on one of the cathedral lamps, hanging from a long chain, anchored high above the church pews. Galileo watched as the lamp swung back and forth. Normally the lamp was stationary, but it had been removed from its usual resting position and was hanging free. The swinging chandelier gave the bored university mathematics student an idea. As the air moved the lamp first one way and then another, Galileo began to notice something about the length of the swings and the amount of time it took to complete each swing. He did not have a clock or watch with which to time the swings, so he felt his wrist for his pulse. He had previously timed science experiments using his pulse during his medical studies.

After several minutes of observation, he came to a conclusion. When he later wrote down what he had discovered, he stated it in simple terms, writing

This fresco shows Galileo observing the movement of a pendulum in the Cathedral of Pisa. In 1583, Galileo articulated the idea of pendulum motion, after watching a swinging chandelier in church.

that "whatever the length of the pendulum swing, the time taken to complete the swing is the same."[9] Without realizing it, Galileo had articulated a new law of physics, known today as the law of the pendulum's periodic swing. At the time of his discovery, Galileo was still in his late teens.

Test Your Knowledge

1 All aristocratic Italian boys were expected to
a. receive a formal education.
b. find a wife.
c. follow in their father's given profession.
d. learn how to recite poetry.

2 When Galileo was 13, his father sent him to a school run by
a. priests.
b. nuns.
c. monks.
d. the pope.

3 Every Italian gentleman was expected to know which of the following languages?
a. Italian and English
b. Italian and Latin
c. French and Latin
d. Greek and Latin

4 Galileo's father wanted him to become
a. a politician.
b. a medical doctor.
c. a banker.
d. a lawyer.

5 Who was Euclid?

   a. An ancient Roman warrior who invented a
      defense strategy

   b. An ancient Latin philosopher who developed
      modern-day sociology

   c. An ancient Greek mathematician who
      invented modern geometry

   d. An ancient Greek scientist who discovered
      many planets and constellations

ANSWERS: 1. a; 2. c; 3. d; 4. b; 5. c

A
New
Direction

Galileo's fascination with the swinging lamp at church led him to experiment with models. After Mass, he went back to his cousin's house, where he was staying at the time, and began building desktop models of swinging objects, using string and weights. Observing as closely as he could, he timed the swings of his miniature "lamps." Such experiments were not common during his time. Rarely did a scientist test his theories and observe the results, but Galileo knew he was thinking about something that no one else had ever thought of. Before he came to a conclusion too soon, however, he wanted to see if his theory was true in every case. He constructed several different pendulums, using string and bobs, or weights. He changed the size and weight of the bobs and even varied the length of the strings. He later described his experiment:

> I took two balls, one of lead and one of cork, the former more than a hundred times heavier than the latter, and suspended them by means of two equal fine threads, each four or five cubits long [six or seven feet]. Pulling each ball aside from the perpendicular, I let them go at the same instant, and they . . . passed beyond the perpendicular and returned along the same path. These free goings and returnings repeated a hundred times showed clearly that the heavy body maintains so nearly the period of the light body that neither in a hundred swings nor even

in a thousand will the former anticipate the latter by as much as a single moment, so perfectly do they keep step.[10]

Time after time, Galileo continued to record the same results. For two bobs of different weights, swung from strings of the same length, the time taken to complete a swing was the same for each weight used. It would be years later before he fully understood the practical significance of his discovery. A pendulum, however, would serve as an excellent tool for building an accurate clock.

Although Galileo's tabletop experiments were simple, using only thread and weights, they were important and groundbreaking. He may have been the first scientist ever to conduct experiments in the study of motion. In addition to their immediate implications, the experiments also proved something else to Galileo—that experimentation was the only way of finding out whether an idea about something in nature was right or wrong. Galileo was creating a new way of looking at scientific problems. In doing so, he was helping to create a whole new field of science—the study of physics.

A NEW FIELD OF STUDY

Galileo was only 19 years old when he conducted the pendulum experiments. He was in the third year of his studies at the University of Pisa. He was proving to be a brilliant student. His studies took up much of his time and interest, and through his studies, he developed a keen love of and fascination with mathematics, especially geometry. He was also developing his own, unique approach to his education. For one thing, he was becoming extremely opinionated. Galileo would study the texts, such as the writings of the ancient Greek philosopher and scientist Aristotle, as all of his fellow students did. Galileo did not automatically accept the conclusions and theories that Aristotle promoted, however, because Aristotle never experimented. To Galileo, Aristotle had never proved anything. For this reason, it became important to the young Italian student to question the theories of Greek scholars such as Aristotle.

For many of Galileo's fellow students, as well as his professors, questioning the work of such an important early scholar was unacceptable. They knew Aristotle and others had used logic to determine what they thought about the world around them, but Galileo became convinced that logic, although important, was not enough. Experimentation was the key. As a result, Galileo often argued with others around him. Many times, both during professors' lectures and outside the lecture hall, he would argue, sometimes getting into loud disputes. During these exchanges, young Galileo would "become excited and raise his voice, loudly disputing the views of his colleagues and lecturers."[11] He spent so much time arguing with others, he was given the nickname "*Il Attaccabrighe*," Latin for "The Wrangler."

Despite his passion for arguing, Galileo remained a respected and well-liked student at the University of Pisa. The young mathematics student was capable of great charm. He was obviously intelligent, took his studies seriously, and was quick with his answers. It might have seemed strange, then, to his fellow students and professors when, in 1585, Galileo left the university before finishing his course of study in mathematics. He had spent four years at the university—two studying medicine and two studying mathematics—when he returned to Florence to live with his family. His father simply could not afford to support his son's studies any longer, but Galileo's time at the university had not been wasted. He had been an excellent student and scholar. He had made friends with fellow students, many of whom came from influential and important families, providing him with possible connections for the future. He had also gained a reputation in academic circles beyond Pisa. When he returned to Florence, he soon established "a reputation among Florentine mathematicians and philosophers." [12] From 1585 until 1589, Galileo earned his living, small as it may have been, privately tutoring students in mathematics. It was work he would continue, on and off, for the next 25 years. For a while, he tutored students at the Vallombroso Abbey. From time to time, he gave public lectures about geometry.

A MEETING OF GREAT MINDS

Despite the fact that he was no longer a student of mathematics at Pisa, Galileo did not give up his studies in geometry. He began to closely read the works of another great ancient Greek scholar, Archimedes, who lived during the third century B.C., about a century after Aristotle. Archimedes's work greatly impressed Galileo. He became convinced that Archimedes was the great scientist that Aristotle had not been. This third-century genius was an inventor, a philosopher, and one of the greatest mathematicians of the ancient world. His studies led him to use what today is known as calculus. Unlike Aristotle, Archimedes's theories had proven true. He is perhaps most famous for his discovery of the law of displacement. This law states that when "a solid object is submersed in a fluid—for example gas or liquid—the weight of the fluid displaced is equal to the apparent loss of weight of the object."[13] One story explained how Archimedes came to his important discovery while sitting in a public bath. As the story goes, he leaped up and dashed home excited to share his new theory—but he was still naked.

Archimedes was an ancient Greek scientist who Galileo could take seriously. The more he studied Archimedes, the more Galileo admired the ancient Greek thinker. He began to refer to Archimedes as "divine." He wrote of his scientific idol, "Those who read his works realize only too clearly how inferior all other minds are compared to Archimedes and

ARCHIMEDES erfter erfinder fcharpfffinniger vergleichung/
Wag vnd Gewicht/durch außfluß des Waffers.

Galileo read closely the works of Archimedes, who was an inventor, a philosopher, and one of the greatest mathematicians of the ancient world. Archimedes is shown here discovering a method of measuring density using water displacement. The method would become known as the Archimedes Principle.

what small hope is left to anyone of ever discovering things similar to what he discovered." [14] Galileo was so impressed with Archimedes, that, despite being home from the university, he wrote a small book about the Greek scientist. The work was titled, *Il bilancetta (The Little Balance)*. For all his admiration of Archimedes, Galileo knew the ancient Greek scientist's work had been hindered by a lack of scientific devices or instruments. To improve on the work of Archimedes, the young Italian mathematician constructed a miniature set of scales (a little balance) delicately and finely made, to use in weighing the density of metals and liquids. Nothing like it had ever been made for the study of science. Today the device would be comparable to a hydrostatic balance.

For years, Galileo continued teaching students privately, but it was not the work he wanted to do. He yearned, instead, to teach mathematics at an important school or university. His age was a problem, though, for he was still a young man in his early 20s. In addition, he had not finished his degree. Still, in 1587, a teaching position at the University of Bologna became available, following the death of the priest–professor who held it. Galileo was desperate to gain the position, but he needed support from someone recognized in the world of mathematics. So he went south to Rome to win the support of one of the most famous Italian mathematicians at that time, a Jesuit named Christopher Clavius. Clavius taught at the College of Rome and was highly regarded as a mathematician. He was known as the "Euclid of the Sixteenth Century."[15] As a student at the University of Pisa, Galileo had studied geometry from textbooks written by Clavius.

When Galileo arrived in Rome, he carried with him a letter from his former geometry professor, Ostillo Ricci. The letter would serve as the young mathematician's introduction to Clavius. After arriving at the great mathematician's apartment in the Vatican, Galileo was invited in. There, before him, sat the famous Jesuit teacher and mathematics scholar:

> The young scientist was ushered into a cluttered office, books piled one upon another, astrolabes, compasses, and quadrant strewn about, and in the center, a short, stout Bavarian with a heavy accent, a close-cropped snowy goatee, and a four-pointed beret above his ruddy, round face. Clavius greeted Galileo warmly. To Galileo's surprise, he seemed to have none of the pretensions of a great man. More important, he treated his visitor as a scholar.[16]

As the two mathematicians—the elder Jesuit and the younger Italian—sat down together, Galileo presented Clavius with some of his latest mathematical work. Clavius was interested and intrigued by this eager young student of geometry. For two months following their meeting, the two men shared

Archimedes and the Crown of Gold

No ancient writer had inspired young Galileo more than the great Greek scientist Archimedes. This genius of the ancient world left a legacy in the sciences that included studies in astronomy, physics, chemistry, mechanics, engineering, motion, and a host of other areas. His personal writings and experiments told the story of an exciting life of discovery. Sometimes, however, separating the factual tales of the life of Archimedes from the great scientist's legend was difficult. One such story involved a king and a gold crown.

According to a famous legend, Archimedes was summoned by his patron, King Heiro, the ruler of Syracuse, on the Mediterranean island of Sicily. The king had just received a new gold crown made by a skilled goldsmith, but King Heiro was skeptical about his crown. He did not believe the royal symbol was made of pure gold. He feared that he had been cheated by the goldsmith. The king wanted

Archimedes to determine, once and for all, the purity of the crown, putting the king's fears to rest.

Archimedes was unsure how to prove the matter, without destroying the crown in the process. Aware of the properties of different metals, the great Greek scientist came upon an answer. Archimedes was aware that gold had a greater density than other metals. The density of a metal, as well as other substances, caused that substance to be heavier or lighter, depending on the specific metal. Lead was a highly dense metal, compared to gold. In scientific terms, density is determined by dividing an object's volume into its mass. By this equation, "if an object occupies a large space and has a small mass it is not very dense."*

For Archimedes, determining the crown's mass would be a simple procedure. The tricky part would be figuring out the crown's volume. Because it was not a geometric shape, like a cube or a ball, Archimedes did not know how to figure out the crown's volume. He had to figure out what to do without destroying the crown in the process. Then, the great mathematician devised a solution:

He would submerge the crown in water and then do the same with an equal mass of pure gold. The amount of water displaced each time could then be calculated. If the same amount of water was displaced, then the density of the metal in the crown would have to be equal to the density of pure gold and the crown would be genuine. If the amounts were different, the crown could not be made of pure gold.**

Archimedes found a solution that was nothing short of brilliant. When the water displaced by the crown and a mass of gold of the same weight as the crown were compared, the result showed King Heiro exactly what he wanted to know. Indeed, the amounts of water displaced were different. The goldsmith had tried to cheat the king by using silver, which is lighter, less dense, than gold.

Despite the details of this amazing story, Galileo did not believe it. He did not believe Archimedes could have used water to determine the small difference in density between gold and silver. The Greek mathematician would have needed a more refined method, a device to measure the tiny differences in density. This story was one of the driving forces behind Galileo's construction of his "little balance."

* Michael White, *Galileo Galilei: Inventor, Astronomer, and Rebel*. Woodbridge, CT: Blackbirch Press, 1999, p. 21.
** James Reston, Jr., *Galileo, A Life*. New York: HarperCollins Publishers, 1994, p. 18.

their ideas on mathematics, but the meeting in the Vatican did not bring Galileo the recommendation he had wanted. Father Clavius did not write a letter proposing Galileo for the mathematics post at the university. The position went instead to Antonio Magini, an instructor who was nine years older. Magini, a mathematician from the Italian city-state of Padua, had already published several books. Galileo's failure to win the Bologna teaching position was disappointing. He was becoming concerned about his future as a scholar, teacher, and scientist. For the moment, he seemed doomed to remain nothing more than a private tutor, living on meager funds, and watching the academic world of university teaching from a distance, but Galileo was not a quitter. He would continue to compete for his place in the scholarly world of mathematics and science. One day his drive would pay off. Five years later, in fact, when he and Magini were again up for the same mathematics post, Galileo would be ready.

Test Your Knowledge

1 Galileo may have been the first scientist ever to conduct experiments in the study of
a. weightlessness.
b. the planets.
c. motion.
d. gravity.

2 Galileo helped to create a whole new field of science known as the study of
a. astronomy.
b. biology.
c. chemistry.
d. physics.

3 How old was Galileo when he conducted his pendulum experiments?
a. 17
b. 19
c. 16
d. 18

4 To Galileo, Aristotle had never proved anything because
a. he never experimented.
b. he never graduated from college.
c. he was not a mathematician.
d. he did not understand the laws of physics.

5 Archimedes is perhaps most famous for his discovery of the law of

a. motion.

b. relativity.

c. gravity.

d. displacement.

ANSWERS: 1. c; 2. d; 3. b; 4. a; 5. d

New Posts, New Obligations

Galileo had failed to receive the mathematics position at the University of Bologna, but he would not have to wait long before another appointment came his way. In the meantime, he experienced other successes. His hydrostatic balance was introduced in academic circles, helping to make Galileo famous throughout

Italy. He also wrote an article in which he presented a theory stating that every object has a "center of gravity." In addition, he continued to lecture publicly whenever possible.

During such lectures, he sometimes spoke not only about mathematics, but also about literature. Late in 1588, he was asked to deliver a lecture that combined both topics into one speech. A group of wealthy Florentines invited Galileo to speak on the subject of mathematics and a popular literary work of the Renaissance, *The Inferno*. It was an epic poem written by Dante Alighieri, the great fourteenth-century Italian poet. In his poem, Dante had described hell as a place of descending circles. Galileo was asked to use mathematics to determine the size and dimension of hell. It was a curious topic, but one Galileo took seriously. The lecture was a success and Galileo became more popular than ever, in Florence and beyond. These advancements in scientific knowledge and lecture successes also helped to advance Galileo's career.

Galileo also received help from a wealthy supporter he had only recently met, the Marquis Guidobado del Monte, a wealthy Italian aristocrat who enjoyed the study of science. He considered himself an amateur engineer and philosopher. With his money, he helped to support the study of science. The marquis was so impressed with Galileo's *Il bilancetta* that he began campaigning on Galileo's behalf. He tried and failed to capture a mathematics position for his young friend at the University of Padua, but when a position became open at the University of Pisa, the marquis succeeded. In 1589, at the young age of 25, Galileo began his career as a professor of mathematics.

For Galileo, the appointment was a mixed blessing. Teaching at a university was certainly more prestigious than barely making a living as a private tutor—and the teaching position did pay more money. Still, the young mathematician's salary was low, 60 crowns a year, only one-thirtieth the amount paid to the highest-paid professor of medicine at the University of Pisa. It was a cruel fact for Galileo that, during the Italian Renaissance, mathematics professors were not paid well. Their work was thought of as almost unimportant. They were considered about as important as those who taught astrology. In fact, just about the time Galileo took the position at the University of Pisa, another mathematics professor retired. His salary, even after teaching for 30 years, was only twice that of young Galileo, who had just started teaching.

To make matters worse, Galileo did not get paid if he ever failed to deliver one of his lectures, even if he was sick. Still, the appointment was a start, and Galileo took advantage of the opportunities it brought him. Controversy was never far away, however. While his scientific work sometimes brought him criticism, on occasion Galileo also went against the policies of the university. For example, it was standard practice at the time for professors at the University of Pisa to wear togas, in the style of the ancient Greeks and Romans. Galileo did not like wearing a toga, because it often got in his way during experiments. He finally refused to wear one, choosing to wear his regular clothes instead. He offended his fellow professors by calling the toga "the disguise of the empty-headed."[17] In response, university officials fined him, depriving him of even more of his meager university wages.

NEW EXPERIMENTS

Despite all of his difficulties, Galileo was finally teaching at a university. In this academic setting, he was soon involved, once again, in scientific study and experimentation. He continued his studies of motion. He soon wrote a small book in Latin titled *De Motu* (*On Motion*). The work was really a series of lessons, probably intended to be used as part of a textbook, but Galileo never published the material. In fact, it was published some 300 years after Galileo wrote it. In the pages of *De Motu*, Galileo continued his objections to some of Aristotle's ideas on motion. One of Aristotle's theories especially troubled Galileo. The famous Greek philosopher had written that objects fall faster when they are heavier. Galileo, through observation, had come to know better. Once, when caught in a hailstorm at the university, he noticed that the hailstones struck the ground at the same speed regardless of their different sizes. The great Aristotle was wrong and Galileo was desperate to prove he knew better than Aristotle. In his frustration, he wrote, "Ignorance of motion is ignorance of nature."[18] Galileo, however, needed to figure out exactly how to prove Aristotle wrong.

According to one story, Galileo did, in fact, come upon an answer. Aristotle had written that "a one hundred pound ball falling from a height of one hundred cubits [about 150 feet] reaches the ground before another of one pound has descended a distance of one cubit."[19] Galileo would test the theory using cannonballs, but he had to find a place where he could drop them from a height of 150 feet. He chose the Tower of Pisa, already an important landmark in Pisa. The leaning bell tower was perfect for Galileo's experiment. Aristotle had written of dropping balls a distance of 150 feet and the tower stood just over 180 feet in height.

Galileo announced to everyone at the university that he intended to perform an experiment to prove Aristotle wrong. He even advertised his intentions to the general public. On the day of the public show, a large crowd—including townspeople, professors, and students—gathered below the tower to witness the demonstration. With confidence, Galileo began the long climb up inside the tower with the help of two assistants. The assent proved more difficult than he had imagined:

The climb was nerve-racking. To reach the top, he had to walk hundreds of worn and slippery steps, winding round in a steep spiral staircase inside the stone walls. By the time he reached the last step, he was sweating and weary. But, he had a job to do. Spurred on by his anger and frustration, he climbed on to the bell tower high above the upper platform of the tower. It leaned to one side at a frightening angle. He only just managed to ignore his feelings of dizziness and pressed on to the highest point.[20]

When, at last, Galileo appeared at the top of the tower, he heard a shout from the crowd below. Many were excited about the spectacle they were about to witness, and most probably expected to watch Galileo's experiment fail miserably. After all, this young, brash mathematics professor could not possibly know more than the great Aristotle. Galileo and his two assistants, according to the story, had carried balls of different sizes, weights, and materials to the top of the tower. Some of the balls were made of "lead and ebony, perhaps even of gold and porphyry [crystaline rocks] and copper."[21]

The high tower platform of the Leaning Tower of Pisa is shown here. Also visible are two stones of approximately the same size as those used by Galileo for his experiment on free fall.

Standing at a towering height equal to 18 stories above the anxious crowd below, Galileo instructed his assistants to place two cannonballs of different weights on the tower's edge. The mathematics professor held out his hand to test the direction of the wind, and found that there was very little breeze. At his signal, two assistants released the cannonballs

Did Galileo Really Drop Balls from the Tower of Pisa?

Galileo's experiment in which he dropped balls of different weights from the Leaning Tower of Pisa is perhaps one of the best-known stories from his life. There are some historians, however, who believe the experiment never happened. Galileo never wrote specifically about the unique experiment in his books, pamphlets, or notes. Some believe that, because he was a man who wanted everyone to know about his experiments, he would not have failed to mention such a dramatic and public test. There are those who believe a similar experiment did take place, but that it was carried out by Dutch mathematician Simon Stevinus, who lived at the same time as Galileo.

Some historians, however, do give credit to the story of Galileo's dramatic experiment. In his writings of later years, Galileo referred to dropping objects from towers. He seemed to refer indirectly to the Pisa experiment in *Dialogue Concerning the Two Chief Systems of the World,* a work written 30 years later. In an even later work, written during his final years, Galileo addressed the mistaken theory of Aristotle and experimentation with balls dropped from towers:

> I say, that the balls reach the ground at the same time. In doing the experiment, you will find that when the heavier mass touches the ground the lighter is two fingers away. Now you are stressing my minor mistake while forgetting about the big one of 99 cubits by Aristotle.*

Of course, regardless of whether the Pisa experiment actually took place or not, Galileo's theory did prove Aristotle wrong. What Galileo could not control in the experiment was air resistance. A larger ball would experience more air resistance because of its size than a smaller ball, even if the smaller ball was of the same weight. Air resistance is what causes a feather to float down to the ground instead of hurtling down like a lead ball. Galileo understood the issue of air resistance. He knew that, if any two objects were dropped in a vacuum, where no air existed, they would fall at exactly the same rate. With no way of eliminating air resistance, Galileo's experiment nearly always resulted in one ball hitting the ground a fraction of a second before the other.

Galileo was not the only scientist to perform experiments with falling objects, but only two or three people had done so before him. Fifty years after Galileo's experiment, Irish scientist Robert Boyle repeated a similar test on falling objects and confirmed the validity of Galileo's results. Four hundred years after Galileo's Pisa experiment, another test of dropping objects of different weights was performed. This time, the place was not the Leaning Tower of Pisa, but on the Moon. In 1969, after American astronauts landed and walked on the Moon's surface, astronaut Neil Armstrong dropped a hammer and a feather at exactly the same moment. On the airless surface of the Moon, the two objects landed in the dusty lunarscape at precisely the same moment. Although no living scientist doubted Galileo's theory by the twentieth century, Armstrong proclaimed, "You see, Galileo was right!"**

* James Reston, Jr., *Galileo, A Life*. New York: HarperCollins Publishers, 1994, p. 32.
** Ibid., p. 31.

at exactly the same moment and watched as the pair of weights hurtled down to the ground below. Galileo had theorized that the two weights would strike the ground at the same time, but in fact, the heavier cannonball hit the ground a fraction of a second—a couple of inches—ahead of the lighter ball. Those in the crowd who had not believed in Galileo's challenge to Aristotle were pleased. They thought Galileo's theory had been proven wrong, but for many, including Galileo, the results of the experiment had proven him correct. The tiny difference in time between the landings of the two balls was the result of air resistance, something that could not be controlled. Galileo had, indeed, proven Aristotle's theory wrong.

Galileo's experiment helped to spread his reputation further, but his new fame came at a cost. He was becoming increasingly unpopular with his fellow professors. Many thought he was too egotistical and that he did not take others seriously. In part, they were right. Galileo was not intimidated by those who were older than he or had more experience. Galileo was becoming a man who did not always live within established rules or even take rules

Galileo's experiment from the top of the Leaning Tower of Pisa disproved Aristotle's theory that objects fall faster when they are heavier. Two cannonballs of differing weights, when dropped from the same distance, traveled at the same speed.

seriously. When an older professor tried to talk down to him, Galileo spoke out against him. Galileo was bright, witty, and argumentative. He dressed sloppily and was unafraid of authority figures. Sometimes he even laughed at them. Above all, however, Galileo was unimpressed with his colleagues. They were not actively seeking new answers in the name of science, something Galileo was beginning to do. Because of his outspoken behavior, the young mathematician did not last long at the University of Pisa. He was hired in 1589 for a three-year term. In 1592, when his term was up for renewal, he was not rehired. Years later, in 1610, he would return to the university to take up the post of chief mathematician. Meanwhile, the 18 years between teaching assignments would bring many changes to the life of Galileo Galilei.

Test Your Knowledge

1 During public lectures, Galileo sometimes spoke
not only about mathematics, but also about
a. literature.
b. religion.
c. science.
d. poetry.

2 *The Inferno*, Dante's famous epic poem is about
a. the end of the world.
b. hell.
c. the Sun.
d. all of the above.

3 How old was Galileo when he began his career
as a professor of mathematics?
a. 22
b. 42
c. 35
d. 25

4 From how high above the ground did Galileo
conduct his experiment at the Leaning Tower
of Pisa?
a. 11 stories
b. 24 stories
c. 18 stories
d. 14 stories

5 Galileo became chief mathematician at the
University of Pisa in what year?
   a. 1160
   b. 1610
   c. 1560
   d. 1615

ANSWERS: 1. a; 2. b; 3. d; 4. c; 5. b

An Eye to the Heavens

For three years, while teaching at the University of Pisa, Galileo had been underpaid and underappreciated. By 1592, when his contract was not renewed, it was time for him to move on. That year, he set his sights on a more prestigious professorship. An important academic position, the mathematics chair, had opened up in the late summer of 1592 at the University of Padua, in northeast Italy, near Venice. The university, the second oldest in Italy, was one of the most important institutions of learning in all of Europe. Its academics placed it in competition with such important universities as those in Oxford, England, and Paris, France.

The mathematics chair position at Padua was a highly regarded academic post. It was, in fact, such an important position, that the university had left it open for four years, in order to find just the right candidate. Even as Galileo showed an interest in the Padua post, however, another mathematician was also interested—Magini, to whom Galileo had lost the Bologna post five years earlier. This time, Galileo was determined to win the coveted Padua placement.

Galileo had his supporters. As before, the Marquis del Monte spoke on his behalf. Because Padua lay within the Republic of Venice, the Venetian senate would decide who to hire for the Padua post. Galileo even left Pisa, "packing all his possessions in a box weighing less than one hundred pounds," and headed for Venice.[22] When Galileo appeared before three representatives of the Venetian senate, two were immediately impressed with him. Galileo was presented to the senate as a favorite choice. When the senators cast their ballots, they accepted Galileo for the open post by a vote of 149 to 8. His reputation as a professor who challenged Aristotle was an important factor in the decision of university officials. The mathematics chairperson they were seeking to replace had also been a challenger of Aristotelian thinking.

Galileo's appointment at Padua was an exciting advancement for him. The pay and prestige at Padua would be far greater than they had been at the University of Pisa. He would receive 180 gold crowns annually, three times his previous salary. The money was important. Galileo's father had died in 1591, and this loss placed a new burden on the mathematics professor. Because he was the oldest son, he was expected to help provide money for his family. On his meager wages at the University of Pisa, he could barely survive on his own. He desperately needed a better paying university post, and he had found such a post at the University of Padua.

The fall semester at the university opened on Saint Luke's Day, October 18, 1592. Galileo was granted time to get his life in order and complete his move from Pisa before he began teaching. He had been hired for a four-year term with an additional two years as an option. Galileo was excited about the challenges and opportunities that lay ahead of him. One of the most important tasks for him that first semester was a lecture he was required to deliver to his fellow professors. This was an expectation for all new faculty members at the University of Padua. On December 7, Galileo stood before his new academic colleagues in the university's Great Hall, the Aula Magna, and delivered his lecture in Latin. He had worked on it for weeks. That day, as he spoke, he used few notes, having memorized nearly all his text. He had even practiced the gestures he would use during the speech. The lecture was a rousing success and was well received. At last, it appeared that Galileo had found just the academic home he had been looking for. Indeed, his arrival in Padua marked the beginning of an 18-year career at the university. Galileo would later describe these years as the "best eighteen years of his life."[23]

THE BEST YEARS

Galileo was now 28 years old. Padua was his new academic home and the opportunities he found there seemed endless. The intellectuals at the University of Padua were much more open to non-traditional ways of thinking than those at Pisa. It was much easier for Galileo to pursue his work and be accepted by his colleagues at the University of Padua. He soon settled down comfortably and "got himself a small house for a home, not far from the most famous church [and monastery] of Santa Giustina."[24] He made friends with the local church abbot who provided him with "a few necessary utensils and pieces of furniture, like beds, chairs and similar things, for which he had little need."[25]

The money he made teaching at Padua allowed Galileo to help his family. He paid his sister Virginia's dowry—the money she brought to her marriage. He provided support for his mother and 16-year-old brother, Michelangelo. Galileo also provided the funds to support his other sister, Livia, who was living at a convent until she married.

Galileo thrived at the University of Padua and among intellectual circles outside the university.

Galileo may have been small in stature, but his scientific wisdom was vast. While he was teaching at the University of Padua, Galileo's students built this rostrum for him, so that they could see their diminutive professor better while he was teaching.

Soon after arriving in Padua, he developed a close friendship with local, wealthy aristocrat Gianvincenzo Pinelli. Pinelli lived in one of the grandest manor houses in Padua, where he kept a personal library of some 80,000 books. He gave Galileo complete and unlimited access to his library. Pinelli, an intellectual, invited Galileo to join the Pinelli Circle, one of the most important intellectual societies in Padua. At society meetings, Galileo engaged in academic conversations and friendly debates. It was through the Pinelli Circle that Galileo met some of the most influential men of northern Italy. The friendship formed with Pinelli would later pay off dramatically for Galileo.

During his years in Padua, Galileo also began a relationship with a young woman named Marina Gamba, "a fiery beauty from the back streets of San Sofia."[26] When they met, Marina was 21 and Galileo was 35. They never married. In fact, they never even lived in the same house, but they carried on a love affair for ten years. During those years, Marina and Galileo had three children. The first, Virginia, was born in 1600. During Marina's first pregnancy, Galileo moved her into a house close to his own in Padua. The last of his children, Vincenzio, the only boy, was born in 1606. Whether Galileo was a loving parent to his children or even a devoted partner to Marina is unclear, but when Galileo left Padua in 1610, to take a post as the chief mathematician in the ruling court of Cosimo de' Medici in Florence, the two lovers finally parted company.

While Galileo's personal life had its ups and downs during his years in Padua, his professional life continued to prosper. He continued his study of motion, experimenting by rolling balls down ramps or chutes rather than just dropping balls from high places. These experiments allowed him to more clearly understand the natural law of acceleration. He also spent time studying ballistics, the science of projectiles, such as balls fired out of cannons. By experimenting with cannons and firing cannonballs, he came to realize that two forces were at play. First there was the velocity of the cannonball caused by the explosion of the cannon. Next there was the cannonball's tendency to fall back to the earth because of gravity. Through this work, he determined that, for a cannonball to be fired to its maximum distance, the cannon should be placed at a 45 degree angle.

From this work, he was also able to design and produce various military instruments, including his

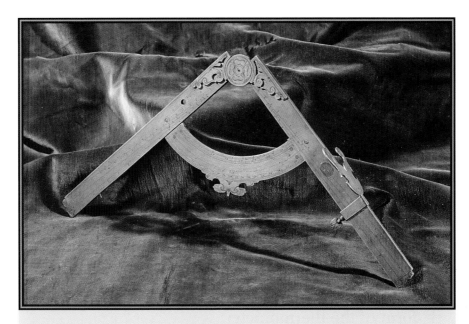

During his years at the University of Padua, Galileo continued experimenting. His experiments led him to produce various military instruments, including the geometric compass shown here.

"military" or "geometric" compass. This device "bore many scales and helped to solve a large number of mathematical and geometrical problems."[27] It was a handheld instrument that performed many of the same tasks as a modern pocket calculator. With this instrument, artillery soldiers could perform quick calculations to determine the ratio of a cannonball's weight to its size. They could also measure the slope or height of a defensive wall. The military compass sold so well, Galileo could not keep up with the demand. He was forced to hire workers to make the compasses. While the device was a money-maker for Galileo, he actually made more money through sales of a booklet that explained how the geometric compass could be put to practical use. During this same productive period of Galileo's life, he invented a device to measure the body temperature of patients in hospital. He called the medical instrument a thermoscope. It was an early form of the thermometer.

TOWARD THE HEAVENS

While teaching at the University of Padua, Galileo became extremely interested in the study of astronomy. In 1597, he read studies done by Polish astronomer Nicolaus Copernicus, who had lived decades before Galileo's birth. One of the theories Copernicus emphasized was his heliocentric theory, which placed the Sun at the center of the solar system. (Aristotle, of course, as well as other ancient philosophers and scientists, had placed Earth at the center of the solar system, with the geocentric theory.) Although Copernicus was dead, his works had been published by another astronomer, a German man named Johannes Kepler. Galileo wrote to Kepler, telling him he agreed with Copernicus. For the moment, however, Galileo did not make his agreement with Copernicus public knowledge. The Copernican system of placing the Sun at the center of the solar system was not accepted by the Roman Catholic Church. Church leaders believed in the geocentric theory of Aristotle and Ptolemy, an ancient scientist who had lived during the second century A.D. To challenge the geocentric theory was to go against church theology and teaching. Such a challenge could result in a charge of heresy, which, even during the enlightened period of the Renaissance, could result in death. The Catholic Church's view did not stop Kepler from writing and publishing his views on the heliocentric theory, but he was a German scientist, living far away from Rome, the center of power for the Roman Catholic Church. Galileo, on the other hand, lived in the shadow of Rome. So, in 1597, when Kepler sent Galileo a manuscript in which he disagreed with the geocentric theory, Galileo quietly read it and privately endorsed it. Publicly, however, Galileo remained silent about his skepticism concerning his personal views in support of the heliocentric theory.

Seven years passed, and, in 1604, an event took place in the heavens that Galileo could not ignore. On October 9, a new star appeared in the night sky.

Air Conditioning and Arthritis

Because Galileo spent much of his time studying, teaching, experimenting, and inventing, he frequently remained indoors, but he was also a lover of nature. He often took long walks up and down the sloping hills of northern Italy. In 1593, following one of his long hikes across the Italian countryside, Galileo, then 29 years old, had a near-death experience that changed his life.

He and a few friends had spent a long summer's day on a lengthy hike. The hikers reached the little town of Costazza, where a wealthy lawyer lived in a handsome estate nestled in the Tuscan hills. Galileo and his companions were welcomed into the lawyer's home and offered food and drink. Famished and thirsty, the guests ate too much and probably drank far too much wine. The men soon laid down to rest.

The lawyer's home had a unique cooling system. Similar to other homes nearby, a shaft had been

The phenomenon was actually an exploding star, known today as a supernova. The appearance of the new star caused an immediate reaction in the academic community. Aristotle had written that the heavens were fixed, unchanging, and perfect. The

carved into the hillside where an opening was made into a cool, underground cavern that was fed by a stream. Chilly air escaped through the tunnel into the house, keeping it cool, even on a hot day. Galileo and his friends slept near the tunnel opening. When they awoke, they were all suffering from painful muscle aches and arthritis, brought on by the cool, humid air. All of them became violently ill, and one of Galileo's friends died. Galileo developed a violent cold that dragged on for several days. When he left the villa, he was still so ill he had to be carried back to Padua in a litter, or a cart.

While Galileo survived these attacks, his decision to sleep next to this primitive air conditioning system would affect his health throughout his later years. For the rest of his life, he was plagued by painful outbreaks of arthritis.

Catholic Church had accepted this view, but in light of the new star, no one could argue that the heavens had not changed. Even before the explosion of this 1604 supernova, other new stars had been observed. One such star had come into view when Galileo was only a small boy, in 1572. Once again, nature had proven Aristotle wrong.

Test Your Knowledge

1 The mathematics chair position at the University of Padua had been open for how many years?
a. Four
b. Six
c. Three
d. Five

2 Galileo's pay at the University of Padua was how many times greater than that of his previous position?
a. Four
b. Six
c. Three
d. Five

3 For how many years did Galileo teach at Padua?
a. 16
b. 28
c. 22
d. 18

4 Gianvincenzo Pinelli's personal library housed how many books?
a. 8,000
b. 6,000
c. 80,000
d. 60,000

5 How many children did Galileo and Marina Gamba have?

a. Six

b. Three

c. Four

d. Two

ANSWERS: 1. a; 2. c; 3. d; 4. c; 5. b

Man of
the Stars

The appearance of the supernova in the night sky led Galileo to take up his study of astronomy once again. He began making systematic observations of the heavens, examining the stars to see if any changes had taken place. He gave extremely popular public lectures, speaking out against Aristotle's writings. He also, for the first time, publicly spoke of his support for Copernicus and his heliocentric theory. Some of Galileo's early conclusions and theories would later be proven wrong, but his theory that the new 1604 supernova was located a great distance from Earth was correct. So, too, were other stars much further away than the Moon and the planets. Those who did not agree with these conclusions argued that the new star was not located in the same celestial region as the other fixed and unchangeable stars that already existed. Galileo was certain of his views of the heavens, even without the instruments needed to prove his theories. There was little he could do to prove his theories, however—until he heard about a new invention already in use in Holland.

THE AGE OF THE TELESCOPE

In 1609, Galileo heard, through a friend, about a new invention that immediately fascinated him. Early that summer "a certain Fleming [Hans Lippershey] had constructed an eye-glass by means of which visible objects, though very distant from the eye, were distinctly seen as if nearby."[28] His friend described the instrument, called a "spyglass," to

Galileo, explaining that it was based on the use of two ground lenses, placed at opposite ends of a tube. A person who looked into one end of the tube could see things close up that were actually far off in the distance. The lens was so new, its inventor did not know exactly how it might be used. Lippershey first thought of his spyglass as nothing more than a toy. Perhaps it could be used to view ships as they approached a harbor, thought Galileo. A spyglass in the hands of a city-state at war with another city-state could be used to spot approaching enemy ships that were still a great distance away. After hearing of the new invention, Galileo went home and began designing a spyglass of his own.

Galileo did not realize it at the time, but he was soon in competition with others who were constructing their own spyglasses. He, however, applied his understanding of perspective and optics to his model. The problem with the early spyglasses was their lack of adequate lenses. Most were poorly made, causing the objects viewed to appear blurred. Galileo ground his own high-quality lenses and redesigned the tubing so that light could not get into it. At the time, Galileo did not intend to use his spyglass to view the night sky. In a letter to a brother-in-law, dated August 29, 1609, Galileo wrote about his early work:

You must know, then, that it is nearly two months since news was spread here that in Flanders there had been presented to Count Maurice a spy-glass, made in such a way that very distant things are made by it to look quite close, so that a man two miles away can be distinctly seen. . . . I undertook to think about [how it was made]; which I finally found, and so perfectly that one which I made far surpassed the reputation of the Flemish one. And word having reached Venice that I had made one, it is six days since I was called by the Signoria, to which I had to show it together with the entire Senate, to the infinite amazement of all; and there have been numerous gentlemen and senators who, though old, have more than once scaled the stairs of the highest [bell towers] in Venice to observe at sea sails and vessels so far away that, coming under full sail to port, two hours or more were required before they could be seen without my spy-glass. For in fact the effect of this instrument is to represent an object that is, for example, fifty miles away, as large and near as if it were only five.[29]

In designing his model of the spyglass, Galileo had actually invented a version of the telescope, a modern scientific instrument. Although he originally saw the spyglass as a military instrument or a tool to aid in navigation, it did not take him long to realize its importance as a tool for research. Through his improvements, he had created a powerful viewing device. By making simple changes, he had improved the view through his spyglass. He had also increased the magnifying power, creating not just another spyglass, but something close to a real telescope. Within weeks of writing his letter, Galileo turned his "telescope" not toward the horizon, but into the sky. What he saw amazed him.

One of the first objects in space upon which Galileo focused his new telescope was the Moon. Aristotle had written that the Moon had a smooth surface. Galileo soon discovered otherwise, and he said:

In designing his own version of the spyglass, Galileo actually invented a version of the telescope. A reconstruction of Galileo's telescope is seen here, with the Duomo, Florence's cathedral, in the background.

It is a most beautiful and delightful sight to behold the body of the moon. . . . [It] certainly does not possess a smooth and polished surface, but one rough and uneven, and, just like the face of the earth itself, is everywhere full of [mountains], deep chasms, and [curving shapes].[30]

Word of Galileo's spyglass reached the doge, the ruler of Venice, through a friend of Galileo's, and

Galileo was soon summoned to the Venetian senate to demonstrate his creation. The doge, who had already been approached by a foreigner with his own spyglass, had been disappointed in its quality. The images it produced were fuzzy and the spyglass only magnified objects by three times. Perhaps Galileo's model would prove better, and, indeed, it did. When Galileo brought his spyglass to the doge, it magnified objects by nine times and its view was clear. The doge and the members of the senate were extremely pleased. The Venetian leader offered to purchase Galileo's spyglass, give him a permanent professorship at the University of Padua, and dramatically increase his salary. Of course, Galileo accepted.

During the following months, Galileo spent much of his time looking through his spyglass, doing research. From September 1609 through March of the following year, Galileo used his telescope to examine the heavens in ways that no one had ever been able to do before. For years, Galileo had criticized Aristotle's and Ptolemy's writings about the solar system, but he had never had a scientific instrument with which to prove his objections. The telescope was just such an instrument.

THE STARRY MESSENGER

By March 1610, Galileo published in Venice one of his greatest scientific works, *Sidereus Nuncius, (The Starry Messenger)*. In this wonderful, small book, an excited Galileo began to inform the world of the discoveries he had made while looking into the night sky with this telescope:

> [I have seen many] stars which have never been seen before, and which surpass the old, previously known, stars in number more than ten times. But that which will excite the greatest astonishment by far, and which indeed especially moved me to call the attention of all astronomers and philosophers, is this, namely, that I have discovered four planets, neither known nor observed by any one of the astronomers before my time.[31]

Galileo had actually discovered what we know today to be the moons of the planet Jupiter. With his new telescope, Galileo's horizons had broadened. His fame spread further than he had ever imagined possible. His future at the University of Padua was assured. His salary would ensure financial security for him and his family. Unfortunately things did not turn out as well as he had hoped. The contract he was eventually given by the doge was not as generous as he had been promised. His salary at the university would not increase as much as he had expected, and his contract placed other restrictions on him, which he did not like. Galileo found the terms unacceptable. Discouraged, he began looking for a better offer elsewhere. He made a quick trip to Florence and showed his telescope to the ruler of that city, Cosimo de' Medici. The Medici family was the most powerful, wealthiest, and most influential family in Italy.

Cosimo de' Medici was thrilled with Galileo's demonstration, and was certain "that this amazing device was the greatest invention of mortal man." [32] He appointed Galileo as the chief mathematician and philosopher to his court. He agreed to all of Galileo's terms. The great scientist did not want to lecture publicly. He wanted all the time he needed to conduct experiments and publish his findings: "I wish to gain my bread by my writings, which I would always dedicate to my Serene Master." [33] For his presence in the court of Cosimo de' Medici,

Dissatisfied with the reception his telescope
had received from the ruler of Venice and the
members of the Venetian senate, Galileo brought
his invention to Cosimo de' Medici, the ruler of
Florence, shown here. Medici was so thrilled with
Galileo's invention, he appointed Galileo as the
chief mathematician and philosopher to his court.

Galileo was contracted at a salary of 1,000 gold crowns a year. This amount, a sum three times that of any artist, scientist, or engineer employed by the Tuscan court, would make Galileo the highest-paid official in Cosimo de' Medici's court. In honor of his new patron, Galileo named his newly discovered Jupiter moons, "the Medicean stars." He also dedicated *Sidereus Nuncius* to Cosimo de' Medici.

Galileo would finally be able to fill his days just as he wanted. No longer would he be bothered with having to lecture or prove himself to university officials and colleagues. With his new telescope, Galileo would be able to prove that Aristotle and his old, long-accepted scientific theories were wrong. He could also prove that Copernicus was right. Galileo believed that all things had finally come together for him. He was sure his authority would be recognized by even his greatest critics and skeptics—that nothing could possibly stand in his way. He could not have been more wrong.

Test Your Knowledge

1 What event caused Galileo to take up his study of astronomy, once again?

   a. The acceptance of his views by the Catholic Church

   b. The appearance of the supernova in the night sky

   c. The acceptance of his views by the people

   d. All of the above

2 In designing his model of the spyglass, Galileo had actually invented a version of

   a. the telescope.

   b. the camera.

   c. the magnifying glass.

   d. the compass.

3 One of the first objects in space upon which Galileo focused his new telescope was

   a. Saturn.

   b. the stars.

   c. the Moon.

   d. the Sun.

4 When Galileo brought his spyglass to the doge, it magnified objects by how many times?

   a. Five

   b. Seven

   c. Three

   d. Nine

5 Galileo discovered the moons of which planet?

a. Saturn

b. Jupiter

c. Mars

d. Uranus

ANSWERS: 1. b; 2. a; 3. c; 4. d; 5. b

A Controversy of Ideas

Galileo received the offer from Cosimo de' Medici to join his prestigious court in July 1609, but he was not able to make all the arrangements to move to Florence until September 1610. With his move from Padua to Florence, he and the mother of his three children went their separate ways. His world was becoming quite different from the one he had experienced at the University of Padua for 18 years. He was a middle-aged man, now 45 years old. His work at Padua had become burdensome, even frustrating. There he had performed for students, colleagues, and administrators, trying to please them all. He wrote of such obligations saying, "I have to consume many hours of the day—often the best ones—in the service of others."[34] In the court of Cosimo de' Medici, he would only have to keep one man happy—the grand duke himself. He was also appointed as first mathematician at the University of Pisa, but he did not have to teach, or even work at the university.

That same month, Galileo was back at work with his telescope, and he soon made another dazzling discovery with his new scientific instrument. He observed an object in space that had been identified as a star, often called the morning star or evening star, because it was visible in both the East and West, close to the horizon, at both times of the day. Through his observations, Galileo soon realized he was looking at a planet. The planet, he observed, had phases, periods when the planet either appeared to grow or shrink, similar to the Moon.

His observation of Venus and its phases helped provide Galileo with further proof that Earth was not at the center of the solar system. The phases of Venus did not all fit within a month, the amount of time required for the Moon to experience its full cycle. The phases of Venus took 18 months. The orbit of Venus, if around Earth, was much further from Earth than Aristotle had determined. In other words, Galileo's observations proved that Venus was closer to the Sun than to Earth, indicating it orbited the Sun instead of Earth. He also observed the rings of the planet Saturn with his telescope, but he saw them as two bodies of light on opposite sides of the planet. His telescope was not powerful enough to see the lights as rings. Galileo's discoveries further validated his telescopic observations of the heavens, but those discoveries would eventually bring trouble for Galileo.

A FATEFUL TRIP TO ROME

By the spring of 1611, Galileo had been working on his astronomical studies for a year and a half. In his mind, he had made great strides toward reducing the value of Aristotle's findings, while building up

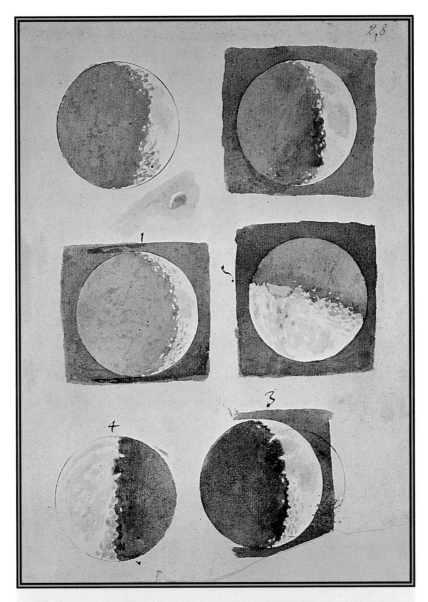

These illustrations of the phases of the Moon were made by Galileo Galilei. When he observed the planet Venus through his telescope, Galileo realized that Venus too, had phases, much like the Moon.

his own reputation and that of Copernicus. He lectured occasionally, and his talks captivated his listeners. That spring, his fame was as widespread as ever, but Galileo was not completely satisfied with the effect his work was having on bringing change to the Catholic Church. He decided it was time for him to pay an official visit to Rome, the center of Roman Catholic power, to demonstrate his scientific findings. He hoped to convince skeptical leaders— including the pope himself—of the need to change the Catholic Church's position on several of its doctrines that conflicted with his scientific discoveries.

His visit to Rome could not have gone better. As Italy's most famous and successful scientist, he was well received everywhere he went in the city. He met with the city's most important and powerful church leaders. Among them was Robert Cardinal Bellarmine, papal secretary of state, one of Rome's leading religious thinkers. Galileo also gained an audience with Pope Paul V, a great honor, for the pope did not grant many such audiences. Galileo did not spend all his time courting church leaders in Rome, however. He also took his telescope on tour all over the city. With his own personal enthusiasm,

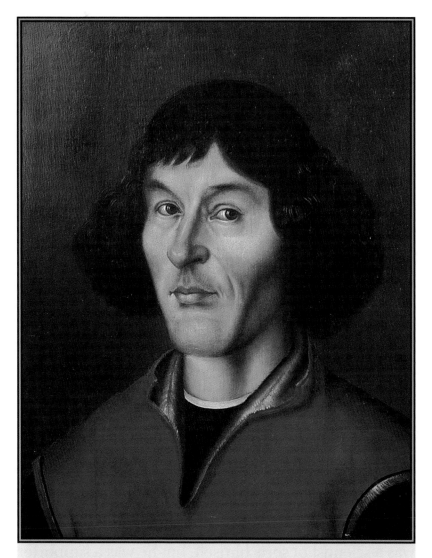

Polish astronomer Nicolaus Copernicus, who had lived decades before Galileo's birth, is shown here. One of the theories Copernicus emphasized was his heliocentric theory, which placed the Sun at the center of the solar system. Galileo's astronomical studies supported this theory.

he set up his demonstrations "in lovely gardens of old palaces, showed his discoveries to large numbers of enthusiastic people and 'converted unbelievers one after the other.'"[35] Success followed Galileo everywhere he went throughout the city of Rome. One cardinal even suggested to Cosimo de' Medici that "a statue [should] be erected to him on the Capitol to honor his excellence and valor."[36]

With success, however, also came jealousy. While some officials appeared to accept Galileo's ideas, others did not. They considered him a threat to the longstanding traditional beliefs of the Catholic Church. By 1612, a group of Galileo's opponents had formed to speak out publicly and write in opposition to his teachings. That year, a German Jesuit named Christopher Scheiner published a book in an attempt to destroy Galileo's reputation and diminish support for his scientific claims. Scheiner was a scientist of sorts himself, but he was a supporter of Aristotle. He, too, owned a telescope which he pointed to the stars, but he saw things differently.

Galileo, through his studies, had observed dark places on the Sun's surface, which he called "sunspots." This observation was unacceptable to

Scheiner, who believed in a perfect universe as a sign of God's handiwork. Sunspots would indicate an imperfection, which would violate Aristotelean thinking. While Scheiner, too, had observed dark spots on the Sun, he claimed that they were tiny planets passing close to the Sun's surface. Galileo knew better. He soon responded to Scheiner's book with a paper titled *Letters on Sunspots*, published in 1613. While the work destroyed the claims of the German Jesuit clergyman, it also represented the first time Galileo had written publicly in support of the Copernican view (heliocentric theory) of the solar system. To make his book available to more people, Galileo had it published in Italian, the common language. At that time, most scholarly works were written in Latin. The book caused an immediate uproar in Rome.

Galileo had challenged the theology of a Jesuit cleric. The Jesuits of the Renaissance were very powerful. They often served as the chief advisors to the Catholic Church on questions of theology, doctrine, and religious education. Reacting to what they saw as a direct challenge to one of their own in a published work, the Jesuits soon turned against

The Faith of Galileo

Clashes sometimes take place between religion and science, even today. Some people and their religious ideas seem at odds with the findings and positions taken by scientists. There are ongoing arguments between religious conservatives who believe in the biblical concept of Creation and those in the arena of science who support the theory of evolution. This conflict between religion and science is not new. It has been around for hundreds of years. It even took place during the life of Galileo.

Galileo worked hard for many years to develop accurate scientific theories. Sometimes those theories were unacceptable to the religious leaders of his time, leading to serious clashes between the scientist and the leaders of the Roman Catholic Church.

Without question, Galileo was a very religious man. As a student of university education, he would have received a certain amount of religious training. Many of the universities in Italy, as well as across Europe during the Renaissance, were operated by the Catholic Church, but Galileo was also a believer because of his scientific work. Through his studies of the natural world, including his observations of space, Galileo "saw signs of a Supreme Will and Power, inscrutable but perfect."*

From time to time, however, his experiments and their results caused a conflict "between his reasoning as a scientist and his loyalty to the Church."** Galileo came to understand that some doctrines of the Catholic Church, regarding things in the world of science, were incorrect, ignorant, and wrongheaded. This realization did not cause him to abandon the Catholic Church. Instead, as a faithful Catholic, Galileo wanted to be part of the process of helping church leaders learn their errors and be able to change their theology and beliefs to match with his scientific findings. He always viewed the Catholic Church's ability to change with optimism. Certain leaders within the Catholic Church did not want to change, however, even when confronted with the facts—making things difficult for Galileo. No matter how much evidence he might present to powerful Catholic leaders, some did not want to see it or face change. At those times, clashes often took place between the world of science and religion.

* Michael White, *Galileo Galilei: Inventor, Astronomer, and Rebel.* Woodbridge, CT: Blackbirch Press, 1999, p. 51.
** Laura Fermi, *Galileo and the Scientific Revolution.* New York: Basic Books, Inc., 1961, p. 82.

Galileo. Even some Jesuits who had previously given their support to Galileo, later turned against him.

AN ULTIMATE SHOWDOWN

Between 1613 and 1615, events began to point to an ultimate showdown between Galileo and the Catholic Church. In 1613, Galileo received word from Father Benedetto Castelli, a friend. He said that Cristina di Lorena, one of the duchesses in the Tuscan court, had spoken in favor of Aristotle's view that Earth did not move in space, but sat motionless. She believed this view was in agreement with the Bible. Galileo responded with his *Letter to Castelli*, which he sent not just to his friend, but also to others. In the letter, he wrote about his views on the clash between science and religion. He wrote a similar letter to Duchess Lorena in which he emphasized his faith in God, God's nature, and the laws he established at Creation. In that letter, he wrote from the heart of a Christian scientist:

> I think in the first place that it is very pious to say and prudent to affirm that the holy Bible can never speak untruth—whenever its true meaning

is understood. But I believe nobody will deny that it is often very abstruse [difficult to understand], and may say things which are quite different from what its bare words signify. . . . For the Bible is not chained in every expression to conditions as strict as those which govern all physical effects; nor is God any less excellently revealed in Nature's actions than in the sacred statements of the Bible. . . . But I do not feel obliged to believe that that same God who has endowed us with senses, reason, and intellect has intended to forgo their use and by some other means to give us knowledge which we can attain by them. He would not require us to deny sense and reason in physical matters which are set before our eyes and minds by direct experience or necessary demonstrations.[37]

Galileo's letters were meant to explain his views on his faith and his science. While the highest officials in the Catholic Church did not question their content, others did. One angry official sent a copy of his *Letter to Castelli* to representatives of the Inquisition. The Inquisition was a Roman Catholic tribunal for the discovery and punishment of heresy, a crime punishable by death.

When representatives of the Inquisition became involved in the controversy swirling around Galileo, events began to take a serious and dark turn. The Inquisition had been established during the Middle Ages as a means of trying heretics, those whose religious ideas were dramatically different from those of Catholicism. By Galileo's time, the Inquisition had changed, somewhat. About 20 years before Galileo was born, representatives of the Inquisition had been ordered to lead the way in the Catholic Counter-Reformation. The Catholic Church was being highly criticized during the early 1500s and many thousands of Catholics were leaving to join other Christians known as Protestants.

These Protestant dissenters believed the Catholic Church had strayed from the true path of Christ's teaching and needed to be reformed. Catholic leaders had responded in a heavy-handed fashion, unwilling to tolerate critics. Critics were sometimes arrested, tried, and condemned to death, usually by being burned at the stake. The Catholic Church exerted its power by censoring any thought or practice it thought of as a threat to Catholicism. By the seventeenth century, members of the Inquisition were serving as the high court of the Roman Catholic Church. With Galileo's ideas representing an immense challenge, members of the Inquisition began taking a closer look at his teachings. This was, indeed, a serious matter for Galileo. If the Inquisition resulted in Galileo being summoned to explain himself, he might be tortured as a means to force him to give up his unacceptable ideas.

BEFORE THE INQUISITION

By December 1614, the controversy surrounding Galileo expanded. That month, a priest named Thomas Caccini began speaking against Galileo publicly from the pulpit of a church in Florence. In his sermons, the priest spoke out against science. He called mathematics an art used by Satan. He proposed that mathematics should be banned from all Christian countries. He called Galileo an "enemy of the true faith."[38] The following year, he would testify before the Inquisition against Galileo. By the spring of 1615, church leaders in Rome believed it was time to bring Galileo to the Vatican to question him about his religious and scientific beliefs. Several important leaders of the Catholic Church were convinced that Galileo would have to choose between his faith and his belief in science.

Later, in 1615, Galileo did appear before the Inquisition. While many of the inquisitors were against him, he did have some supporters. One such supporter, Cardinal Robert Bellarmine, was much more open minded than many of his colleagues. In a letter he wrote at the time to another church official, he stated his views of the science Galileo supported:

> I say that if a real proof be found that the sun is fixed and does not revolve around the earth, but the earth around the sun, then it will be necessary, very carefully, to proceed to the explanation of the passages of Scripture which appear to be contrary, and we should rather say that we have misunderstood these than pronounce that to be false which is demonstrated.[39]

The majority of those involved in the Inquisition, however, were largely interested in condemning Copernican theory, and they intended to convince

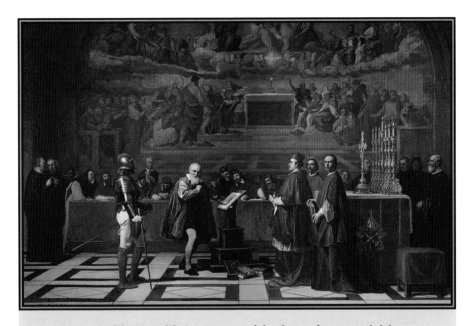

In 1613, Galileo Galilei appeared before the Inquisition to defend his belief that the Sun, not Earth, was at the center of the solar system. By early 1616, the Inquisition condemned Copernicus's heliocentric theory as heresy.

Galileo to do the same. When Galileo did appear before the Inquisition, he desperately wanted to explain himself to his accusers. He defended his scientific views, and they listened intently. Galileo was, of course, not someone they could easily disregard. He was known as an extremely talented and intelligent scientist, but they remained unconvinced. By early 1616, members of the Inquisition condemned Copernicus's heliocentric theory as heresy, and ordered Galileo "not to hold, teach, or defend it in any way whatever, either orally or in writing."[40] Even his supporter Cardinal Bellarmine tried to convince Galileo to cooperate. In the end, the Italian scientist did just that. With his life perhaps on the line, he gave in. He promised to drop his support of Copernicus.

Galileo was crushed by the pressure that had been placed on him by the Inquisition. He had planned to write a book comparing the Ptolemaic and Copernican views of the universe, but he was forced to give up that plan. He had tried for years to convince ignorant clerics of the truth of his scientific views. He had failed. Instead they had won. The Catholic Church had silenced the voice of one of the most brilliant scientists in history.

Test Your Knowledge

1 How old was Galileo when he joined Cosimo
   de' Medici's court?
   a. 45
   b. 54
   c. 47
   d. 56

2 Galileo observed that the phases of Venus took
   how many months?
   a. 16
   b. 12
   c. 18
   d. 24

3 Galileo had observed dark places on the Sun's
   surface, which he called
   a. "sun shadows."
   b. "sunspots."
   c. "sun shades."
   d. "sun flares."

4 The Inquisition had been established during the
   Middle Ages as a means of
   a. finding a new pope.
   b. making changes in the Catholic Church.
   c. converting people to Catholicism.
   d. trying heretics.

5 The majority of those involved in the Inquisition were largely interested in

a. condemning Copernican theory.

b. supporting Galileo's theories.

c. finding a suitable new pope.

d. changing the Catholic Church.

ANSWERS: 1. a; 2. c; 3. b; 4. d; 5. a

The Trial

A VOICE SILENCED

For two years, Galileo Galilei remained silent, refusing to defy the authority and power of the Inquisition. He had not actually been banned from speaking about Copernicanism, but he had been cautioned to be careful how he spoke on the subject. He could present the

Copernican model as a theory, but he could not teach it as a proven fact. Galileo remained cautious. From 1613, the year he published his *Letters on Sunspots*, throughout the following ten years, he did not publish anything. He was busy with his science. He continued his astronomical studies, designed a special telescope for sailors, and negotiated with Spain "over navigational uses of his astronomical discoveries."[41] Despite his attempts at staying away from controversy, Galileo could not do so forever.

In 1618, the heavens beckoned again. That summer, three comets appeared in the night sky. Galileo was ill at the time and could not observe the comets for himself, but friends told him about them, and the comets greatly excited him. A Jesuit named Orazio Grassi soon wrote about the comets, claiming they streaked through the sky in a straight line, proof against Copernicanism. He published his work under the pen name Lothario Sarsi. In his book, *The Astronomical and Philosophical Balance*, Grassi was highly critical of Galileo's earlier writings and views of astronomy. Galileo felt that many of Grassi's accusations were unfair. Although Grassi

During the summer of 1618, three comets appeared in the night sky. A Jesuit named Orazio Grassi soon wrote about the comets, claiming they streaked through the sky in a straight line, proof against Copernicanism. The comet Halley, as seen in Australia, is shown here.

had the backing of many church astronomers, Galileo could not remain quiet. He began writing *The Assayer,* one of his best scientific works, in response. Galileo took several years to write his work, finally publishing it in 1623.

Today some of the views of comets expressed by Galileo in his book are known to have been wrong. That does not, however, diminish the most important point Galileo was making. He wrote *The Assayer* to express his opinions of Grassi and others like him who were misusing science. His words were direct and to the point. In his book, he was extremely witty and even sarcastic. He addressed Grassi (who wrote using the name Sarsi) directly: "The crowd of fools who know nothing, Sarsi, is infinite. Those who know very little of philosophy are numerous. Few indeed are they who really know some part of it, and only One knows all." [42] Galileo, in fact, was so harsh and undiplomatic with Grassi, that he probably offended even some who might have agreed with him. The book took away some of his support.

A SUPPORTER BECOMES POPE

Even as the book was being printed by his supporters in the Lincean Academy, an important event took place that gave Galileo new hope for his future studies. The pope died, and was replaced by one of

Galileo's supporters, Cardinal Barberini, who was appointed Pope Urban VIII. He and Galileo had shared many conversations on science topics. Pope Urban was highly enlightened and had even written a poem in honor of Galileo. With Pope Urban leading the Catholic Church, Galileo hoped that perhaps the way would be cleared for his scientific ideas. The new pope even invited Galileo for an audience. For the great astronomer, things were looking better.

Galileo, despite some illness and his increasing age, managed to make a trip to Rome during the spring of 1624. He hoped Pope Urban would help him overturn the decision of the Inquisition, forbidding him to teach Copernicanism. The meeting went well. Galileo's old friend, now the leader of the Catholic Church, was glad to see him. He praised *The Assayer*, which Galileo had dedicated to Cardinal Barberini. Galileo brought the pope a wonderful scientific instrument, called a microscope. It was a new invention, but not one created by Galileo. The two old friends sat down together, and Galileo displayed images of gigantic insects under his microscope.

Galileo soon discovered, however, that the atmosphere had changed. Pope Urban would not

In his days as cardinal, Pope Urban VIII (shown here) had always been very supportive of Galileo and his scientific theories. With Pope Urban leading the Catholic Church, Galileo hoped that his scientific ideas would perhaps be more widely accepted by the Catholic Church.

authorize Galileo to return to his teachings on Copernicanism. The Inquisition's decision would not be overturned. In his new role as leader of the Catholic Church, Pope Urban VIII showed another side of himself:

> Urban VIII, the Pope, . . . was to reveal less attractive traits that had not been evident in the cardinal. Shrewd, with an extremely high opinion of himself, avid for power, jealous of his authority, he was so ambitious both for himself and for his family that his nepotism was to become proverbial. The Barberinis' revenues and their power became enormous.[43]

In his new role, Pope Urban VIII knew he now spoke for all believers in the Catholic Church. While he might have been able, as a cardinal, to listen to and support Galileo's theories, as a pope, he could not give him his full support. He authorized Galileo to discuss Copernicanism, but only as a theory, not as fact.

Galileo soon returned to his home in Florence, ready to write publicly again on heliocentric theory. He may have believed that Pope Urban VIII had given him greater permission to write on the subject than had actually been intended. Nevertheless the great astronomer was soon busy at work writing one of his greatest scientific works, *Dialogue Concerning the Two Chief World Systems.* It is often simply called *Dialogue.*

DIALOGUE

Perhaps Galileo was so eager to begin writing in 1624 because he saw his health declining in his later years. He was already 60 years old, and his health was not good. Even as he began writing his important scientific work, he took years to complete it. Sometimes he laid it aside and concentrated on his experiments and astronomical studies. At other times, he was simply too ill to write. On one occasion, he became so ill, he nearly died. By 1630, he had finished writing the book. He presented the manuscript to officials of the Catholic Church in Rome before publication. He dedicated the book to his old friend, Pope Urban VIII. Galileo hoped his work would be quickly accepted by the Catholic Church, but censors held up publication of the book for two years. During that time, Galileo was forced to defend his work. Finally they allowed the book's publication, but told Galileo to change his introduction and the manuscript's final paragraphs. They wanted him to make certain that he presented the Copernican view as a theory, one of many ideas that might be studied about the makeup of the universe. By 1632, Galileo published his work in Florence. As with earlier works, *Dialogue* was published in Italian, not Latin.

Even today, Galileo's *Dialogue* remains one of the great works of scientific writing. It was structured as other literary works sometimes were in his day. Although the book focused on Galileo's personal and professional scientific beliefs, it centered on a conversation between three Italian gentlemen. Two of them, former friends of Galileo's, had died—a Florentine named Salviati and a Venetian named Sagredo. Years earlier, Galileo had been a regular guest at Salviati's magnificent villa in the Tuscan hills outside Florence. Galileo had performed several of his astronomical experiments at Salviati's house. Both Salviati and Sagredo had been intelligent men who had a keen interest in science and learning.

In the book, both men were presented as highly intellectual and open minded. The third gentleman in the book was a supporter of Aristotle's. He did not accept any idea that he could not read about in an ancient text, especially one written by Aristotle. The idea of experimentation and observation meant nothing to him. Galileo displayed his prejudice toward this man's views by naming him "Simplicio," meaning the gentleman was "simpleminded" or a "simpleton."

By writing his controversial views in support of Copernicus in this way, Galileo could avoid stating his ideas directly. In the structure of a three-person conversation, he could put words in the mouths of others, while keeping himself at a distance. When Salviati's character refers repeatedly to "our friend the Academician," however, it is understood that he is referring to Galileo. The conversational approach also made the book easy for the average reader to understand. Through these three characters, Galileo's *Dialogue* covered nearly every subject the great Italian scientist had ever studied. He even included the results of his studies on motion, which he had begun some 40 years earlier. The main theme of the book, however, was the discussion and comparison of the two systems describing how the universe is structured, the Copernican and the Aristotelian or Ptolemaic systems. Galileo put Salviati and Simplicio on opposite sides throughout the book. As Galileo presented the two men, Salviati was always right and logical, while Simplicio was always misguided and even wrong. Sagredo provided further argument against Simplicio.

Why a Trial?

Galileo's *Dialogue* exploded into a controversy within months following its publication. Although the work was popular with readers and brought Galilieo much praise, officials of the Catholic Church responded harshly. Galileo was shocked at the response to his book. He believed he had written about the Copernican system without going beyond the limits the advisors to the Inquisition had placed on him almost 20 years earlier. He had presented the manuscript to Catholic Church officials in Rome before its publication, and they had approved it. What suddenly was the problem with his book and its content? Why was a trial before the Inquisition suddenly necessary?

The answers are not easy. For hundreds of years following Galileo's trial, the court documents were sealed and kept secret. Even today, however, with those documents available, historians are uncertain why the Catholic Church turned so violently against Galileo. One possible answer focuses not on the content of Galileo's book, but on his old friend Pope Urban.

It appears that Pope Urban was extremely angered by Galileo's writing. Although he had once been a supporter of the great Italian scientist, Pope Urban became one of Galileo's most bitter enemies. Historians believe that Pope Urban became so angry, because he thought Galileo had tricked him. When the two men met in Rome, before Galileo wrote *Dialogue*, they had discussed the issue. The pope believed he had made the ground rules clear for Galileo to write about Copernican theory. He had told Galileo to present the theory as one of the possible explanations of the universe. He had told him to also present Aristotelian or Ptolemian theory, as well.

Galileo had done both throughout the pages of his book, but he had presented a distorted view of the two theories. Support for Copernicanism was everywhere in *Dialogue.* The only advocate for Aristotle was Simplicio, whose arguments in favor of the geocentric theory were consistently mocked and destroyed. From the pope's view, Galileo had not balanced his approach to both systems.

Pope Urban may also have been angered by something else Galileo may have done in his *Dialogue.* The other two characters in Galileo's book, Sagredo and Salviati, were based on two men Galileo had known during his life. Perhaps the character of Simplicio was based on a particular person, as well. Certainly Galileo intended Simplicio to represent the misplaced scientific ideas held by everyone, scientists and members of the clergy alike, but Pope Urban may have come to believe that Galileo modeled Simplicio after him. He may have become convinced that Galileo was specifically mocking him and the Catholic Church. In doing so, Galileo was making fun of the one of the most powerful institutions of seventeenth-century Europe. While it is unlikely that the great Italian scientist had Pope Urban in mind specifically for the Simplicio character, his intent did not matter. Galileo had offended his friend, and he would soon be forced to pay the price.

Simplicio was never able to convince Sagredo and Salviati of his position, but the book ended with both intellectuals changing their minds. Galileo did this to convince officials of the Catholic Church, including the pope, to allow him to publish the book.

When Galileo's *Dialogue* was published, it was an instant success. Copies were sold across Europe, and many people considered the book a great work of science. Even the Catholic Church seemed to accept it. One court official to Pope Urban VIII even advised: "These novelties of ancient truths, of new worlds, new systems, new nations, are the beginning of a new era."[44] One reader praised Galileo's book endlessly: "It is full of wonderful, new things, explained in such a way that anyone can understand it perfectly. Wherever I start reading, I can't put it down."[45] The praise Galileo received immediately following the book's publication would soon fade, however, as he began receiving criticism from officials of the Catholic Church. Galileo had presented his views indirectly and with prejudice. He had not presented a dialogue that was balanced in its approach to both Copernicus and Aristotle. He had made those who supported Aristotle look uneducated, unenlightened, and stupid. Church officials, including Pope Urban, were not pleased.

Just months after *Dialogue's* publication, Roman officials ordered the book's publisher to stop selling the work. A few months later, Galileo was called to appear before a court of the Inquisition in Rome. He needed to explain why he had violated his earlier agreement not to write in support of the Copernican system. Pope Urban would preside at the trial. The life and career of one of Europe's greatest scientists was in question.

AN ACCOUNTING

Even before the great scientist's trial before the Inquisition and the pope began, officials of the Catholic Church began treating Galileo harshly. He was 69 years old and in poor health. That year, a plague was ravaging the Tuscan countryside, making travel dangerous. Galileo begged for the trial to be delayed. Pope Urban VIII would not hear of it. He was angry with his old friend. Galileo, according to Pope Urban, had "ventured to meddle with things that he ought not and with the most grave and dangerous subjects that can be stirred up in these

A few months after the publication of *Dialogue,* Galileo was again called to appear before the Inquisition. He was being asked to explain why he had violated his earlier agreement not to write in support of the Copernican system. His trial in 1633 is shown here.

days."[46] He ordered Galileo to come to Rome. When the aged scientist fell extremely ill, he was given time to recover, but, once he was well enough to travel, he would be brought to Rome in chains.

Galileo began to fear for his life. He asked to have the trial held in Florence, where he believed he would face a more open-minded audience. The pope refused. Galileo offered to rewrite *Dialogue* to make it acceptable to the Inquisition. The pope refused. Florentine officials gave little support to one of their most famous citizens. Galileo's old patron, Cosimo de' Medici, had died many years before. Galileo's friends and supporters seemed few and far between.

After months of delays, Galileo finally left for Rome on January 20, 1633. He was so weak from recent illnesses that he had to be carried in a litter, a kind of cart. The trip took three weeks. On Lent Sunday, February 13, he arrived outside the city. Ordinarily, a person awaiting trial before the Inquisition was placed in the Vatican's prison. Given his physical condition, age, and fame, Galileo was allowed to remain in the Tuscan embassy until trial. In exchange, he was ordered not to speak about his case to anyone. For more than four months, Galileo anxiously awaited a decision from the inquisitors regarding his fate.

During those agonizing months, he was questioned several times about his beliefs. By mid-April, he faced the Inquisition directly. He was accused of defying church doctrine and Pope Urban VIII himself by writing and publishing *Dialogue.* That book, he was told, contained heresy by giving support to

Copernican theory. Galileo defended himself, claiming that "by writing this book, I do not think that I was contradicting any injunction."[47] The members of the Inquisition remained unconvinced. By late June, Galileo was brought to a large hall in a monastery, in the center of the city of Rome. He was ordered down on his knees, as the sentence against him was read aloud:

> We sentence you, Galileo, for the things found in the trial and confessed by you, have made yourself . . . vehemently suspected of heresy, namely to have held and believed false doctrine, contrary to the Holy and Divine Scriptures. . . . We are agreeable that you will be absolved provided that first, with sincere heart and unfeigned faith, you . . . curse . . . the above mentioned errors and heresies . . . We order that the book the *Dialogue* . . . be prohibited by public edict. We condemn you to formal prison . . . and we impose on you as salutary penances that for the next three years you say the seven penitential psalms once a week.[48]

Galileo, aged and fearful that he would be killed, agreed to the terms. While still kneeling on the floor, he agreed to "never again say or assert, verbally or in writing, anything that might furnish occasion for a similar suspicion."[49] In his heart, Galileo knew he was turning his back on the truth of his science, but he had just been condemned to prison for the rest of his life. With his confession and promise to remain silent on Copernicanism, Pope Urban VIII finally showed his former friend some kindness. He reduced his prison sentence to house arrest in Florence. Galileo had received a light sentence, and he knew it, but he still emerged from the agonizing trial a broken man.

Test Your Knowledge

1 After his appearance before the Inquisition,
Galileo remained silent for how long?
a. Four years
b. Two years
c. One year
d. Three years

2 With which country did Galileo negotiate over
navigational uses of his astronomical discoveries?
a. France
b. Italy
c. Spain
d. England

3 With Pope Urban leading the Catholic Church,
Galileo hoped that perhaps
a. his ideas would be accepted.
b. he would be appointed to a position in the
Catholic Church.
c. he would be asked to come to Rome.
d. he would write another book.

4 In what language was Galileo's *Dialogue* published?
a. Italian
b. English
c. Spanish
d. Latin

5 When Salviati's character in *Dialogue* refers repeatedly to "our friend the Academician," to whom is he referring?
a. Copernicus
b. Pope Urban
c. Galileo
d. Aristotle

ANSWERS: 1. b; 2. c; 3. a; 4. d; 5. c

The Pendulum Swings

FINAL DAYS

Following his trial and sentencing, Galileo was allowed to live in Siena, in the home of Archbishop Ascanio Piccolomini, a friend, for the remainder of 1633. Archbishop Piccolomini had admired Galileo for many years. Although the great scientist did not

134

know what the future held for him, surely he was saddened by the results of the trial. His sentence of house arrest meant he would never be allowed to visit Florence again, and Galileo knew his conviction was wrong. He knew he held the truth, that the leaders of the Catholic Church were mistaken in their theology, and that scientists everywhere would be reluctant in the future to challenge the traditional authority and power of the Catholic Church. The day he was condemned by the Inquisition was a setback for science. As a result of his conviction, the Catholic Church decided to ban all of Galileo's writings.

By December, Galileo was allowed to return to his home outside of Florence, but an Inquisition guard would be close by at all times. His personal letters were screened. Anyone visiting Galileo had to receive approval from the Vatican. One comfort of returning home was that Galileo would once again be close to his two daughters, who lived as nuns in a local convent. Each girl had been sent to the convent when she turned 16. Galileo moved to the small town of Arcetri, near Florence, in 1631, to be closer to his daughters, but an additional tragedy

Galileo moved to the small town of Arcetri, near Florence, in 1631, to be closer to his daughters. The exterior of Galileo's house in Arcetri is shown here.

soon struck. Just months after his return, one of his daughters, Sister Maria Celeste, fell ill and died. She was only 33 years old at the time, and the loss was devastating for her aged father.

Meanwhile illness continued to affect Galileo's quality of life, but he had been bruised by the Catholic Church, not crushed. As time passed, his natural spark of curiosity and experimentation returned. He studied, painted, and, with no hope of ever being published again, began to write. In the three years between 1634 and 1637, Galileo wrote another great work of scientific literature, *Discourses Concerning Two New Sciences*. Again the pages of his writing presented a conversation between Salviati, Sagredo, and Simplicio, but this time he did not support any controversial scientific theories. He wrote, instead, a book about his motion studies, mechanics, physics, and the nature of matter—the results of a lifetime of study. Although no Italian publisher would publish *Two New Sciences*, Galileo did find a publisher. A Dutch printer named Louis Elzevir, who lived in Holland, put Galileo's work in print in 1638. Holland was a Protestant country, where the Catholic Church had no authority. When

Galileo (right) dictates to his son for his book entitled *Discourses Concerning Two New Sciences*. The book dealt with Galileo's motion studies, mechanics, physics, and the nature of matter.

the book became public, the Catholic Church did nothing to stop it. As one of his final scientific works, *Two New Sciences* helped set the stage for future studies by other scientists. Galileo's life, however, was drawing close to its end.

Galileo never saw or read his last book after it was published. For years, he had suffered from eye problems. Today doctors believe he probably had glaucoma. In 1636, an infection blinded his left eye. Unable to receive proper medical treatment while under house arrest, his condition worsened. By 1638, he lost the remainder of his sight. He took the loss hard. He wrote to a friend:

> Your dear friend and servant Galileo is . . . completely blind; in such a way that the sky, that world and that universe, which with my wondrous observations and clear demonstrations I amplified a hundred and thousand times over what was believed most commonly by the learned of all past centuries, is for me now so diminished and narrowed that it is no greater than what my body occupies.[50]

Despite the loss of his sight, Galileo continued to work. He gave instructions to assistants, who carried out experiments for him. In his final years, Catholic officials lessened the restrictions on Galileo. No guard remained outside his house, and visitors came from far and wide. Friends, well-wishers, aristocrats,

Great Minds Come Together

During the final years of his life, Galileo was still one of the most famous men in Europe, and was still considered one of the great minds of his time. Other great men sought contact with the aged scientist, astronomer, and philosopher before his death. Noted English philosopher and political thinker Thomas Hobbes paid a call to Galileo's house in Arcetri. Hobbes told Galileo that his *Dialogue* had been published in English. Fellow Italian scientist Evangelista Torricelli, who would become the inventor of the modern barometer, also visited him.

One of the most curious visitors was a 29-year-old poet from England. His name was John Milton, and he was touring Europe, seeking new knowledge. He wanted to meet some of the continent's great thinkers and try to understand how they viewed the world. Little is known about his conversation with Galileo, who was nearly 50 years his senior.

When Milton was older and had established himself as a great poet and writer of the great epic poem *Paradise Lost,* he gave a speech before the English Parliament and spoke of Galileo. The topic was the prohibition of books by the Catholic Church. In his address, Milton stated:

> I could recount what I have seen and heard in other countries, where this kind of Inquisition tyrannizes . . . that this was it which had damped the glory of Italian wits, that nothing had been there written now these many years but flattery. . . . There it was that I found and visited the famous Galileo, grown old, a prisoner of the Inquisition for thinking in astronomy otherwise than the [Catholic Church] thought.*

In his own later years, Milton searched, as had Galileo, for knowledge and truth. The two great thinkers were alike in that respect. They were also alike in another way. Just as Galileo had lost his sight during his final years, so, too, did Milton become blind at the end of his life.

* Laura Fermi, *Galileo and the Scientific Revolution.* New York: Basic Books, Inc., 1961, p. 110.

philosophers, and scientists, all came to see Galileo. Then, in late 1641, Galileo contracted a severe fever. For years, he had suffered from arthritis, and painful attacks often struck suddenly. He suffered for weeks until, on January 8, 1642, he died in his sleep, just a few weeks before his seventy-eighth birthday.

When Galileo died, the civic leaders of Florence, the city he considered home, voted to build a monument to honor the great scientist. Pope Urban VIII, still angry at Galileo, denied their request. More than a century would pass before his body would be placed in a grand marble tomb, a fitting burial site for one of the greatest minds in the history of modern science.

AN ABIDING LEGACY

New centuries brought other honors and recognitions of Galileo's scientific discoveries and theories. In 1744, Pope Benedict XIV allowed for the publication of *Dialogue,* the book that had caused Galileo so much trouble in 1632. During the following century, *Dialogue* was finally removed from the Inquisition's official list of banned books. That same year, in 1822, another pontiff, Pope Pius VII, officially allowed the publication of books that taught that Earth revolved around the Sun, the center of the solar system. Seventy years later, Pope Leo XIII even established an astronomical observatory in the Vatican. Though it took centuries, the leaders of the Catholic Church eventually came to acknowledge the validity of Galileo's theories. It was not until the 1960s and 1970s, however, that officials began to take a closer look at the trial of Galileo. Some wanted the Catholic Church to admit it had mistreated the great scientist. By 1979, Pope John Paul II ordered the case against Galileo reopened and his conviction reconsidered. Church officials studied the historical record for years, and finally came to realize their mistakes. Still no apology or reversal of Galileo's conviction took place. Then, in 1992, more than 350 years after Galileo's trial, Pope John Paul II officially announced the Catholic Church's error. Pope John Paul even quoted Galileo's very words when he said, "Holy Scripture and nature proceed equally from the Divine Word."[51]

Today the world of science owes a debt of gratitude to one of its greatest minds, Galileo Galilei. His work in medicine, physics, mechanics, motion,

A telescope, triangle, magnet compass, and pendulum clock belonging to Galileo Galilei are shown here. His work in medicine, physics, mechanics, motion, ballistics, astronomy, and gravity paved the way for the scientists of the future.

ballistics, astronomy, and gravity helped lay the groundwork for future studies. His pioneering efforts in establishing a new approach to the study of science—the scientific method—redefined the way scientists approach complex issues in all of their studies. Galileo's studies were so closely connected to modern science that one cannot help but think that if he were alive today, he might be tinkering with the latest supercomputer—or designing the next spacecraft. Perhaps he would be searching for the newest wonder drug. Surely, just as he had done over the course of his long and fruitful life, he would still be reaching for the stars.

Test Your Knowledge

1 As a result of Galileo's conviction, the Catholic Church decided to
   a. ban all of Galileo's writings.
   b. ban the teaching of any scientific theories.
   c. excommunicate Galileo.
   d. support Aristotle.

2 Anyone visiting Galileo had to receive approval from
   a. Artistotle.
   b. Galileo.
   c. the Vatican.
   d. the governor.

3 What happened to one of Galileo's daughters, just months after his return?
   a. She got married.
   b. She had a baby.
   c. She wrote a book.
   d. She fell ill and died.

4 For years, Galileo suffered from an eye problem that doctors today think was probably
   a. nearsightedness.
   b. glaucoma.
   c. farsightedness.
   d. tunnel vision.

5 Galileo died just a few weeks before which birthday?

a. His seventy-eighth

b. His eighty-seventh

c. His sixty-fifth

d. His seventy-second

ANSWERS: 1. a; 2. c; 3. d; 4. b; 5. a

1543   Polish astronomer Nicolaus Copernicus publishes his heliocentric theory in his book, *The Revolution of Heavenly Spheres.*

1544   Galileo Galilei is born in Pisa, Italy, in Tuscany.

1545   Galileo enrolls as a medical student at the University of Pisa.

1546   Galileo leaves his studies at the university without having graduated; he continues his studies in mathematics and privately tutors students.

1547   Galileo writes his first scientific work, *Il bilancetta,* which gains him the attention of other European scientists and mathematicians.

1544 Galileo Galilei is born in Pisa, Italy, in Tuscany

1548 Galileo accepts a teaching post as professor of mathematics at Pisa University; he begins his studies on motion and teaches against the theories of Aristotle

1609 Galileo constructs his first primitive telescope

1544

1546 Galileo leaves his studies at the University of Pisa without having graduated; he continues his studies in mathematics and privately tutors students

1550 Galileo conducts his legendary experiment by dropping different weights from the top of the Leaning Tower of Pisa

1551 Galileo is appointed professor of mathematics at the University of Padua, where he soon begins a relationship with Marina Gamba; they have three children together

1548 Galileo accepts a teaching post as professor of mathematics at Pisa University; he begins his studies on motion and teaches against the theories of Aristotle.

1549 Galileo writes *De Motu*, which includes his studies on motion and falling bodies.

1550 Galileo conducts his legendary experiment by dropping different weights from the top of the Leaning Tower of Pisa.

1551 Galileo is appointed professor of mathematics at the University of Padua, where he soon begins a relationship with Marina Gamba; they have three children together.

1610 One of Galileo's greatest scientific works on astronomy, *The Starry Messenger*, is published; before year's end, Galileo leaves for Florence where he takes a position as court mathematician for Cosimo II; using a telescope, Galileo discovers the moons of Jupiter

1621 After standing trial before the Inquisition, Galileo is condemned, found guilty, and ordered to remain under house arrest for the rest of his life

1623 Eye infections cause Galileo to lose his sight

1642

1614 Galileo is ordered by church officials to appear in Rome to explain his support for Copernicanism; Galileo agrees not to speak or write on the subject as a fact

1612 Galileo publishes *Letters on Sunspots*, which supports the heliocentric theory of Copernicus

1620 Galileo writes his controversial *Dialogue Concerning the Two Chief Systems of the World*; the book draws the ire of the members of the Inquisition, who summon him to Rome to account for his theories

1642 Galileo dies at the age of 77

1552 Galileo carries out his studies of motion by experimenting with inclines and ramps.

1553 A supernova appears in the night sky, giving Galileo further evidence against Aristotelian theory.

1554 Galileo's first child is born, a daughter named Virginia.

1555 Galileo's second child is born, a daughter named Livia.

1606 Galileo's third child is born, a son named Vincenzio.

1609 Galileo constructs his first primitive telescope.

1610 One of Galileo's greatest scientific works on astronomy, *The Starry Messenger,* is published; before year's end, Galileo leaves for Florence where he takes a position as court mathematician for Cosimo II; using a telescope, Galileo discovers the moons of Jupiter.

1611 Jesuit mathematician and astronomer Father Christopher Scheiner publishes a book on sunspots with which Galileo immediately disagrees.

1612 Galileo publishes *Letters on Sunspots*, which supports the heliocentric theory of Copernicus.

1613 Galileo's work is criticized by Dominican priest Thomas Caccini.

1614 Galileo is ordered by church officials to appear in Rome to explain his support for Copernicanism; Galileo agrees not to speak or write on the subject as a fact.

1618 After three comets appear in the night sky, Galileo returns to publicly present his ideas in support of Copernicus.

1619 Galileo publishes *The Assayer*, which challenge's the Catholic Church's theologies concerning the universe.

1620 Galileo writes his controversial *Dialogue Concerning the Two Chief Systems of the World*; the book draws the ire of the members of the Inquisition, who summon him to Rome to account for his theories.

1621 After standing trial before the Inquisition, Galileo is condemned, found guilty, and ordered to remain under house arrest for the rest of his life.

1622 Galileo's daughter Marie Celeste dies at the age of 33; that same year, Galileo begins writing *Discourses and Mathematical Demonstrations Concerning Two New Sciences*.

1623 Eye infections cause Galileo to lose his sight.

1624 *Two New Sciences* is published in Holland, a Protestant country.

1642 Galileo dies at the age of 77.

NOTES

CHAPTER 1
Early Directions
1. Clarice Swisher, ed., *Galileo*. San Diego, CA: Greenhaven Press, 2001, p. 11.
2. Laura Fermi, *Galileo and the Scientific Revolution*. New York: Basic Books, 1961, p. 5.

CHAPTER 2
Born of the Renaissance
3. Michael White, *Galileo Galilei: Inventor, Astronomer, and Rebel*. Woodbridge, CT: Blackbirch Press, 1999, p. 11.
4. Swisher, *Galileo*, p. 15.
5. White, *Galileo Galilei: Inventor, Astronomer, and Rebel*, p. 11.
6. James Reston, Jr., *Galileo: A Life*. New York: HarperCollins Publishers, 1994, p. 9.
7. White, *Galileo Galilei: Inventor, Astronomer, and Rebel*, p. 11.
8. Ibid., p. 12.

CHAPTER 3
A Searching Mind
9. White, *Galileo Galilei: Inventor, Astronomer, and Rebel*, p. 18.

CHAPTER 4
A New Direction
10. Fermi, *Galileo and the Scientific Revolution*, p. 15.
11. White, *Galileo Galilei: Inventor, Astronomer, and Rebel*, p. 14.
12. Ibid., p. 20.
13. Reston, Jr., *Galileo: A Life*, p. 19.

14. Ibid., p. 20.
15. White, *Galileo Galilei: Inventor, Astronomer, and Rebel*, p. 21.
16. Ibid., p. 22.

CHAPTER 5
New Posts, New Obligations
17. Reston, Jr., *Galileo: A Life*, p. 34.
18. Ibid., p. 30.
19. Ibid.
20. White, *Galileo Galilei: Inventor, Astronomer, and Rebel*, p. 27.
21. Reston Jr., *Galileo: A Life*, p. 30.

CHAPTER 6
An Eye to the Heavens
22. Reston Jr., *Galileo: A Life*, p. 40.
23. Fermi, *Galileo and the Scientific Revolution*, p. 26.
24. Ibid.
25. Ibid.
26. Reston, Jr., *Galileo: A Life*, p. 62.
27. Fermi, *Galileo and the Scientific Revolution*, p. 33.

CHAPTER 7
Man of the Stars
28. Fermi, *Galileo and the Scientific Revolution*, p. 48.
29. Jacob Bronowski, *The Ascent of Man*. Boston: Little, Brown and Company, 1973, pp. 201–202.
30. Ibid., p. 204.
31. Ibid.
32. White, *Galileo Galilei: Inventor, Astronomer, and Rebel*, p. 44.
33. Reston, Jr., *Galileo: A Life*, p. 103.

NOTES

CHAPTER 8
A Controversy of Ideas

34. Reston, Jr., *Galileo: A Life*, p. 84.
35. Fermi, *Galileo and the Scientific Revolution*, p. 74.
36. Ibid.
37. Ibid., p. 79
38. Paul Hightower, *Galileo: Astronomer and Physicist.* Springfield, NJ: Enslow Publishers, 1997, p. 72.
39. Fermi, *Galileo and the Scientific Revolution*, p. 72.
40. Ibid., p. 73.

CHAPTER 9
The Trial

41. Fermi, *Galileo and the Scientific Revolution*, p. 84.

42. Ibid., p. 86.
43. Ibid., pp. 88–89.
44. Hightower, *Galileo: Astronomer and Physicist*, p. 83.
45. Reston, Jr., *Galileo: A Life*, p. 233.
46. Hightower, *Galileo: Astronomer and Physicist*, p. 86.
47. Ibid., p. 90.
48. Fermi, *Galileo and the Scientific Revolution*, p. 97.
49. Ibid., pp. 97–98.

CHAPTER 10
The Pendulum Swings

50. Fermi, *Galileo and the Scientific Revolution*, p. 109.
51. Hightower, *Galileo: Astronomer and Physicist*, p. 100.

Brecht, Bertoldt. *Galileo.* New York: Grove Press, 1966.

Bronowski, Jacob. *The Ascent of Man.* Boston: Little, Brown and Company, 1973.

Fermi, Laura. *Galileo and the Scientific Revolution.* New York: Basic Books, 1961.

Hightower, Paul. *Galileo: Astronomer and Physicist.* Springfield, NJ: Enslow Publishers, 1997.

Mason, Paul. *Galileo.* Chicago: Heinemann Library, 2001.

Reston, Jr., James. *Galileo: A Life.* New York: HarperCollins Publishers, 1994.

Swisher, Clarice, ed., *Galileo.* San Diego, CA: Greenhaven Press, 2001.

White, Michael. *Galileo Galilei: Inventor, Astronomer, and Rebel.* Woodbridge, CT: Blackbirch Press, 1999.

Books

Bendick, Jeanne. *Along Came Galileo*. Sandwich, MA: Beautiful Feet Books, 1999.

Boekhoff, P.M. *Galileo*. San Diego, CA: Gale Group, 2003.

Doak, Robin S. *Galileo*. Minneapolis, MN: Compass Point Books, 2005.

Fisher, Leonard Everett. *Galileo*. New York: Simon & Schuster Children's Books, 1992.

Goldsmith, Mike. *Galileo Galilei*. Chicago: Raintree Publishers, 2002.

McTavish, Douglas. *Galileo*. London: Franklin Watts, 1991.

Nardo, Don. *Trial of Galileo*. San Diego, CA: Lucent Books, 2004.

Websites

Galileo Galilei
http://www.hao.ucar.edu/public/education/sp/images/galileo.html

Galileo-Galilei.org
http://www.galileo-galilei.org

NASA Quest—Galileo Galilei
http://quest.arc.nasa.gov/galileo/About/galileobio.html

PBS.org—Galileo Galilei
http://www.pbs.org/wnet/hawking/cosmostar/html/cstars_galileo.html

University of Missouri at Kansas City—Famous Trials
http://www.law.umkc.edu/faculty/projects/ftrials/galileo/galileo.html

PICTURE CREDITS

Tim McNeese is a prolific author of books for elementary, middle and high school, and college readers. He has published more than 70 books and educational materials over the past 20 years, on everything from Indian legends to the building of the Great Wall of China to a biography of President George W. Bush. McNeese is an Associate Professor of History at York College in York, Nebraska, where he is currently in his fourteenth year of teaching. Previously, he taught middle- and high school history, English, and journalism for 16 years. He is a graduate of York College (AA), Harding University (BA), and Southwest Missouri State University (BA, MA). His writing has earned him a citation in the library reference work, *Something About the Author.* His wife, Beverly, is an Assistant Professor of English at York College. They both love to travel. In 2003 and 2005, they hosted a college study trip for students along fifteen hundred miles of the Lewis and Clark Trail from eastern Nebraska to western Montana. They have two children, Noah and Summer. Readers may e-mail Professor McNeese at tdmcneese@york.edu.